P9-BZY-765

101

QUESTIONS

ABOUT

MUSCLES

TO STRETCH YOUR MIND
AND FLEX YOUR BRAIN

• • • • •

FAITH HICKMAN BRYNIE

• • • • •

TFCB TWENTY-FIRST CENTURY BOOKS

MINNEAPOLIS

The photographs in this book are used with permission of: © The Granger Collection, New York, p. 8 (left); Courtesy of the National Library of Medicine, p. 8 (right); © Gladden Willis, M.D./Visuals Unlimited, p. 12 (left); © Dr. John D. Cunningham/Visuals Unlimited, p. 12 (right); Ivan Rayment, University of Wisconsin, p. 24; © Dr. Don W. Fawcett/Visuals Unlimited, p. 25; © Ken Lucas/Visuals Unlimited, p. 41; © Tom Walker/Visuals Unlimited, p. 42; © Marcus Mok/Asia Images/Getty Images, p. 45; © Bettmann/CORBIS, p. 59; © Franck Fife/AFP/Getty Images, p. 65; AP Photo/ASO/HO, p. 68; © Richard Heathcote/Getty Images for DAGOC, p. 75; W.S. Marras, p. 79; © Jonathan Daniel/Getty Images, p. 84; George El-Khoury, p. 89; © Chuck Swartzell/Visuals Unlimited, p. 101; Allan Mishra, p. 102 (both); © Superstock/Superstock, p. 110; © Arthur Siegelman/Visuals Unlimited, p. 112; Shari Works, p. 116; Mohsen Shahinpoor, p. 139; NASA, p. 143; Vincent J. Caiozzo, p. 147.

Cover: © Boris Lyubner/Illustration Works/Getty Images.

Twenty-First Century Books
A division of Lerner Publishing Group, Inc.
241 First Avenue North
Minneapolis, MN 55401 U.S.A.

Website address: www.lernerbooks.com

Library of Congress Cataloguing-in-Publication Data

Brynie, Faith Hickman, 1946–
    101 questions about muscles : to stretch your mind and flex your brain / by Faith Hickman Brynie.
        p.   cm. — (101 questions)
    Includes bibliographical references and index.
    ISBN-13: 978–0–8225–6380–8 (lib. bdg. : alk. paper)
    1. Muscles—Miscellanea—Juvenile literature. I. Title. II. Title: One hundred one questions about muscles. III. Title: One hundred and one questions about muscles.
QP321.B83 2008
612.7'4—dc22   2006037041

Manufactured in the United States of America
1 2 3 4 5 6 – BP – 13 12 11 10 09 08

CONTENTS

Foreword 7

CHAPTER ONE
23 Questions That Should Come First 11
   Feature: Muscling around the Animal Kingdom 40

CHAPTER TWO
17 Questions about Specific Muscles 44
   Feature: Lance Armstrong and the Tour de France 65

CHAPTER THREE
13 Questions about Muscles and Exercise 69
   Feature: The Straight Scoop on Steroids 84

CHAPTER FOUR

24 Questions about Injuries and Diseases 88

Feature: A Day in the Life of a Physical Therapist 116

CHAPTER FIVE

24 Questions You've Always Wondered About 120

Feature: Muscles in Space 143

In Closing: More Questions Than Answers 148

Glossary 150

Selected Bibliography 155

For Further Information 156

Notes 161

Index 172

ACKNOWLEDGMENTS

The author appreciates the contributions of all those who helped make this book a reality. Much gratitude is due to those teachers whose students provided some of the most thought-provoking questions answered here: Mark Stephansky, Whitman-Hanson Regional High School, Whitman, Massachusetts; Kay Collins, Badin High School, Hamilton, Ohio; and Janet Chahrour, Cincinnati Country Day School, Cincinnati, Ohio.

The author also wishes to thank wellness expert Carol L. Johnson, CHES, CWS, of Apex, North Carolina, for her expert critical review. Special thanks are extended to Douglas A. Syme, Associate Professor, Department of Biological Sciences, University of Calgary, Alberta, Canada. He provided the kind of complete and concise critical review every author dreams of. His guidance at numerous points throughout the research and writing process was invaluable.

Thanks to Geoffrey P. Dobson, Professor of Physiology and Pharmacology, James Cook University, Townsville, Queensland, Australia, for his prompt and cheerful assistance with matters ranging from mitochondria to artificial muscles. Thanks to Robert Nolan,

Behavioural Cardiology Research Unit, University of Toronto, Canada, for his help with biofeedback and heart rate control. Gratitude also to Steven Vogel, Professor of Biology, Duke University, Durham, North Carolina, for his assistance with force, power, and efficiency. Thanks also to Suzanne Schneider, Department of Physical Performance and Development, University of New Mexico, Albuquerque, for her help with "Muscles in Space." The wonderful story of Jan Swammerdam would never have appeared here without the help of biologist and historian Matthew Cobb, University of Manchester, England.

The greatest of all gifts is given by those who support day-by-day a process that is its own reason for being. Thank you, Ann, for being a model of courage and common sense. Thank you, Lloyd, for being more than a pretty face and a great cook. You are my all.

FOREWORD

It cannot any longer be ignored how incomplete our knowledge of what is common to all muscles has been and still is, and how great an area of investigation lies waiting for those who are not shy of work.[1]
—NIELS STENSEN, 1667

Okay, I confess. Before I started working on this book, I had never heard of Jan Swammerdam. If you have, give yourself two points, one for science and one for history. If you haven't, then come with me. We'll explore together one of the most fascinating stories that historians of science have to tell.

Jan Swammerdam was born in Amsterdam in 1637. He trained as a physician, but he never had a "real job." He had serious money problems. He often argued with his family. He had few friends and struggled to find himself, bouncing back and forth between scientific inquiry and mystical reflection. He was, however, a careful investigator and an observer ahead of his time. In an age when everyone else believed that insects had no internal structures, he dissected bees and ants and produced detailed drawings of their organs. He documented the life cycle of a metamorphosing insect from egg to larva to pupa to adult. He showed that the developmental stages were not different animals, as his contemporaries thought, but all the same creature, just in a different form.

Swammerdam studied humans as carefully as he studied insects. He found eggs in the female ovary. He found valves in the vessels that carry lymph, the fluid that bathes all body cells. He proved that an inflow of blood causes an erection in the human male. He was among the first to observe red blood cells. He even discovered what causes a hernia (a condition in which part of the intestine pokes through a hole in the muscles of the abdominal wall).[2]

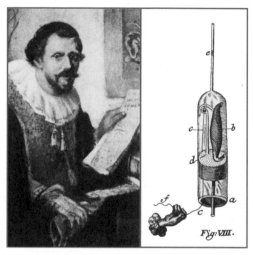

Jan Swammerdam and a drawing from his experiment on muscle volume

Swammerdam wasn't afraid to challenge conventional wisdom. He designed and performed experiments to test the time-honored "truth" that muscles expand when they are active. In Swammerdam's time, most scientists believed that active muscles increased in volume because animal spirits flowed into them through the nerves, which they thought were hollow tubes. This idea had originated more than 1,500 years before in the writings of the Greek physician Galen of Pergamum (A.D. 129–216). No one had tried to find out what the spirits were or how they worked, but few doubted they existed. In Swammerdam's time, only the foolhardy dared question Galen. He and other famous Greeks, including Aristotle, were the undisputed source of truth.

Swammerdam dared to challenge the wisdom of the ancients.

Here's what he did: He removed the thigh muscle from a frog. (If you have ever done this in a science lab, you know that the muscle will contract when you touch it, even though it is no longer hooked up to the animal's blood vessels, nerves, or brain.) He placed the muscle in an airtight syringe. He used a bubble of water at the end of the syringe to measure the muscle's volume in its contracted and relaxed states. What he observed surprised him. The bubble didn't move. Whether relaxed or active, the muscle's volume stayed the same.

Now, perhaps, we come to the reason why I (and maybe you?) had never heard of Swammerdam. *He didn't believe his own results.* Convinced that something must be wrong with his experiment, he explained away his findings. The thigh just wasn't a good muscle to use in showing a change in volume, he decided.[3]

Other scientists of Swammerdam's time and more recent centuries have shown that the Dutchman had the right result, if the wrong explanation. Contracted muscles do not change in volume. If they get shorter, they also get thicker, but the amount of space they take up stays the same.

Swammerdam may have missed the point on volume, but he redeemed himself when he rejected the notion that animal spirits "pump up" muscles. "It cannot be demonstrated by any experiments, that any matter of sensible or comprehensible bulk flows through the muscles. Nor does any thing else pass through the nerves to the muscles," he wrote.[4] The ability of muscles to change shape and exert a force comes from their own internal machinery.

Today scientists can see that machinery using microscopes. They use electronic instruments to measure force, power, and efficiency. We know so much about muscles now that it is hard to imagine a time when we didn't. But does that mean we know all there is to know about muscles? Far from it. As Swammerdam's contemporary Niels

Stensen wrote, "How great an area of investigation lies waiting for those who are not shy of work."[5] In these pages, you'll have a chance to explore what we know (or think we know) and what we are trying to find out about our muscles. You'll read about how protein molecules slide past one another inside individual muscle cells, grabbing and holding on when the muscle contracts. You'll explore how muscles are named and how they work. You'll learn which ones produce the ordinary movements most of us take for granted. You'll find out how exercise affects muscles. You'll learn what can go wrong when the machinery of muscle is damaged. You'll get a glimpse into the world of modern research on muscles where biologists, physicists, engineers and even psychologists probe questions as "Why do muscles tire?" and "Can we make and use artificial muscles to repair, replace, or even improve on the real thing?"

As you read, you'll discover how much and how little we know about muscles. You'll share in the excitement of researchers who are challenging current knowledge every bit as much as Swammerdam did—hopefully without dismissing their own findings. There is much to be learned if (in Swammerdam's words) "we have a mind to observe, very exactly. . . ."[6]

That's what this book invites you to do.

CHAPTER ONE

23

QUESTIONS

THAT SHOULD COME FIRST

*Everything expresses itself in movement, and the ability to
move is one of the qualities that define life.*[7]
—IRWIN M. SIEGEL
ALL ABOUT MUSCLE: A USER'S GUIDE

**What are
muscles?**

Muscles are tissues composed of muscle
cells. The contraction of a muscle may produce a movement—either a voluntary one,
such as kicking a ball, or an involuntary one,
such as the beating of the heart.

Muscles come in three varieties:

- **skeletal:** These are the striated muscles that produce voluntary
movements—movements we can consciously control. (Striations
are alternating bands of light and dark that can be seen when looking at these cells through the lens of a microscope.)

- **cardiac:** Striated but involuntary, this muscle tissue is unique to the heart.
- **smooth:** Also involuntary but not striated, these muscles line the blood vessels, hair follicles, and urinary and genital tracts. Smooth muscle pushes food through the digestive tract.

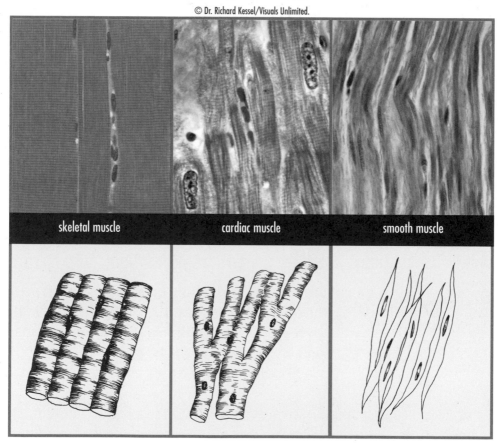

The three types of muscles. The photographs on the top are muscle tissues seen through a light microscope. On the bottom are drawings of the cells.

Individual muscle cells are called fibers or myocytes. (*Myo-* means muscle and *-cyte* means cell.) As the table shows, they vary in size and shape, and they may contain more than one nucleus. (A nucleus is a dense body found inside some, but not all, types of cells.)

CHARACTERISTICS OF MUSCLE FIBERS			
QUESTION	SKELETAL	CARDIAC	SMOOTH
Where are these muscles?	attached to bones	wall of the heart	digestive and respiratory systems and other sites
Are striations present?	yes	yes	no
How many nuclei?	many	one (centrally placed)	one (centrally placed)
What is the shape of the cell (fiber)?	cylindrical with tapered ends	cylindrical	spindle-shaped; elongated and tapered
How big is the cell?[8]	10–100 microns in diameter; 0.79 inches (2 centimeters) or more long[9]	10–50 microns in diameter; 100 microns long	5–10 microns in diameter; 100–200 microns long
Is a nerve impulse required?	yes	beats spontaneously, but speed is moderated by nerves	affected by nerves, hormones, chemicals, and physical stretching
Is the contraction voluntary?	yes	no	no
How fast is the contraction?	fast	fast to moderate	slow (often prolonged and sustained)

What are the functions of muscles?

When you think of muscles, you may think first of voluntary movement, but that's only part of the story. Muscles maintain posture and counteract the effects of gravity. Without them, you'd sink to the floor as soon as you rolled out of bed. Muscles also produce much of the heat that keeps a human body at the temperature of 98.6° Fahrenheit (37° Celsius). In total, your muscles use some 20 to 30 percent of the energy you expend when resting.[10] (The amount of energy you expend at rest is known as your basal metabolism.)

When you shiver in the cold, your muscles burn even more energy to keep you warm. Erector pili, tiny muscles in the skin, cause hairs on the arms and legs to rise when you are cold. That action provides a small insulating effect. It closes the pores of the skin and traps a layer of warm air near the surface. Muscle tissue also stores energy—in the form of glycogen, a compound of the sugar glucose. Muscle also acts as a storehouse for the amino acids that all cells of the body use to make proteins. Proteins are the building blocks of cells, not usually an energy source. But in times of starvation, the body breaks down muscle protein and uses it for energy.

Muscles even affect hormones and mental health. Using the muscles of the face to form a facial expression sends a message to the brain. The brain responds by releasing the appropriate hormone. That's why a good treatment for the blues is smiling—even when you don't want to. The muscle movements of smiling trigger the release of "feel-good" chemicals in the brain.

What kinds of movements do skeletal muscles produce?

Nearly 20 different terms describe the movements that skeletal muscles produce. The table describes some of the major ones.

Some movements are combinations of these major types. For example, circumduction is a combination of flexion, abduction, extension, and adduction. You make that

TYPE OF MOVEMENT	DEFINITION	EXAMPLES
flexion	a bending movement that decreases the angle between two bones	bending the lower leg back toward the back of the thigh; bending at the elbow, moving the hand toward the upper arm
extension	a straightening or stretching movement that increases the angle between two bones	straightening the leg or arm
hyperextension	extension beyond the usual limits	the exaggerated curve in the back of gymnasts; tilting the head far back to look up into the sky
abduction	moving a body part away from the middle of the body	using the muscles of the outer thigh to move the leg away from the body
adduction	moving a body part toward the middle of the body	using the muscles of the inner thigh to pull the leg toward the body
rotation	circular motion around the long, vertical axis of the body or a limb	turning the head from side to side to signal "no"
protraction	moving forward, parallel to the floor	jutting the jaw forward
retraction	moving to the rear, parallel to the floor	pulling the jaw back
elevation	vertical movement	shrugging the shoulders or raising the lower jaw to close the mouth
depression	opposite of elevation; lowering	lowering the lower jaw or the shoulders

movement when you move your entire arm from the shoulder so that the hand traces a circular shape in the air. Some movements are unique to a particular part of the body. Plantar flexion, for instance, is an ankle motion. You make it when you stand on your tiptoes. Dorsiflexion also occurs in the ankles, but in the opposite direction. Raising your toes to balance on your heels requires dorsiflexion. Pronation is the movement that turns the hand, palm down, or rolls the foot inward. Its opposite is supination, which turns the hand palm up or the foot outward.

Even the simplest action may involve many muscles and multiple actions. Can you guess what the drawings on this page show? They show an arm shooting a basketball. It takes dozens of arm, hand, and shoulder muscles to accomplish this action. That's not counting the running of the legs, the movement of the feet, and the twisting of the torso required to get a round ball though a circular hoop.

Muscles of the shoulder, arm, and hand carry out six different actions while shooting a basketball.

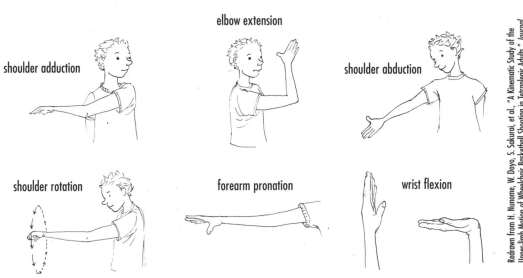

elbow extension

shoulder adduction

shoulder abduction

shoulder rotation

forearm pronation

wrist flexion

Redrawn from H. Nunome, W. Doyo, S. Sakurai, et al., "A Kinematic Study of the Upper-limb Motion of Wheelchair Basketball Shooting in Tetraplegic Adults," *Journal of Rehabilitation Research and Development* (January/February 2002), pp. 63-71.

No. They vary in several ways. One is the arrangement of the fibers. Pennate or bipennate muscles, such as the gastrocnemius (calf) muscle, concentrate large numbers of fibers on a tendon (where the muscle attaches to something else, such as bone). That relays most of the muscle's force directly to the bone. In fusiform muscles, fibers run parallel to the tendon to which they attach, so they concentrate fewer fibers on the tendon and develop less force. An example is the sartorius muscle in the leg.

Muscles also vary in size and shape, depending on their location and function. Compared to muscles in other parts of the body, the muscles of the arms and legs are long and thin. The sartorius, for example, is nearly 2 feet (60 cm) long.[11] The shape of limb muscles allows them to produce the big movements of running a marathon or swinging a bat. On the other hand, short muscles, such as those of the eye, produce tiny movements. More than fifty tiny muscles in the face produce facial expressions of great variety.

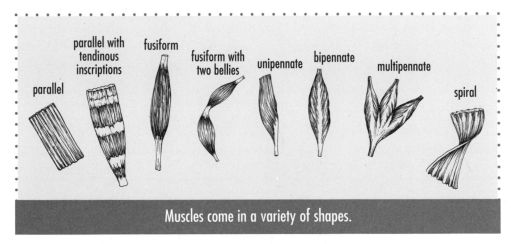

parallel

parallel with tendinous inscriptions

fusiform

fusiform with two bellies

unipennate

bipennate

multipennate

spiral

Muscles come in a variety of shapes.

In contrast, the muscles of the abdomen and back are broad. They form sheets that wrap around the body. They provide protection for the internal organs and keep the body upright. Some muscles, such as the short, flat muscles of the hip, help stabilize the body. Other abdominal muscles are long. The iliocostalis thoracis, for example, runs the length of the six lower ribs and connects with other muscles below and above it. It's the one people are talking about when they remind you to stand up straight.

How do skeletal muscles work?

The connective tissue of muscle extends beyond the muscle fibers to form a round cord or flat band called a tendon or a thin, broad sheet called an aponeurosis. The tendon or aponeurosis binds the muscle to bone, cartilage, fibrous tissue, or another muscle. The skeletal muscles that produce voluntary movements attach to two (or sometimes more) bones. Bones come together at joints. There, strong fibers called ligaments hold them together. Bones act as levers. The pulling of muscles on those levers lets you walk, run, sit, and stand. Bursas are fluid-filled sacks that lie between tendons and the bones beneath them. They cushion the joint. Synovial membranes line the bursas. They produce the lubricant synovial fluid.

When a skeletal muscle contracts, one of its points of attachment—usually the one closer to the center of the body—does not move (or moves only a little). It is called the origin. The other attachment point is farther from the center of the body and more moveable. It is called the insertion. Origins and insertions vary depending on the muscle type and how the muscle is attached to the bones. Some muscles have wide, flat origins. Some attach directly to bone. Others narrow into long tendons that fit into a slot in the bone. Some muscles begin in several places—they have more than one origin—and then attach to a single bone on the insertion end.

Most muscles work in opposing pairs. The agonists, or "prime movers," produce a specific movement. The antagonists are the muscles that oppose the agonists. They make the bones move in the opposite direction. Whether a muscle is an agonist or antagonist depends on the movement being considered. For example, the quadriceps in the front of the thigh are agonists when you straighten a knee. The hamstrings at the back of the thigh oppose them. The hamstrings act as antagonists. The situation reverses when you bend a knee. The hamstrings are the agonists and the quadriceps are the antagonists.

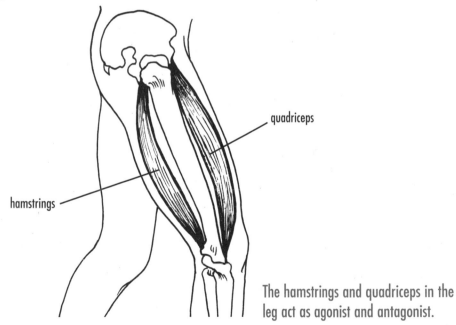

quadriceps

hamstrings

The hamstrings and quadriceps in the leg act as agonist and antagonist.

Muscle actions are complicated. It usually takes more than the agonist and antagonist to produce motion. "Helper" muscles called synergists contribute to any complex motion. For example, the gastrocnemius muscle acts as a synergist to the hamstrings when bending the knee. In addition, stabilizer muscles hold joints in place and the body in position whenever any part moves. In this example, the sartorius and gracilis muscles of the thigh are important stabilizers of the knee when the hamstrings contract.

What do tendons do?

Tendons do a lot more than just hook muscle to bone. They are made of more than 90 percent collagen[12] (the protein that gives elasticity to skin, bones, cartilage, and connective tissue). Tendons are stiff yet pliable. They transfer the muscle's force to the bone and joint during voluntary movement. Furthermore, stretching tendons stores elastic energy within them. (Think of a rubber band stretched between your fingers. When you let it go, it returns to its original shape, releasing a lot of the energy that was used to extend it.) The elastic energy stored in a tendon during one part of a movement makes the next part of the movement more economical, more powerful, and less reliant on muscle contraction. Tendon is an efficient elastic material. It gives back about 93 percent of the work required to stretch it. That's about the same as rubber.[13] So the stretched tendon literally "puts a spring in your step."

Does a muscle get smaller when it contracts?

No. A contracted muscle may change its shape, but its total volume stays the same.

For example, when you "make a muscle" to show off your upper arm, the ends of the muscle pull toward each other. The middle of the muscle gets thicker as a result, but the total size of the muscle does not change. In other cases, an active muscle hardly changes shape at all. An example is pushing against a wall. Or, an active muscle may actually get longer and narrower, as it does when you reach to catch a ball above your head.

How do muscles contract?

The "sliding filament model" explains muscle contraction. Here's how it works.

A single muscle cell or muscle fiber contains many myofibrils. Myofibrils are bundles of filaments that can contract, or shorten. Some are thick and some are thin. Each is made of several proteins. Two of the most important are actin and myosin. Actin is a major component of the thin filaments. The thick filaments contain myosin. Neat stacks of filaments are arranged into functional units called sarcomeres. Each myofibril is many sarcomeres stacked end to end. This repeated structure makes skeletal muscle look striated when viewed through the lens of a microscope.

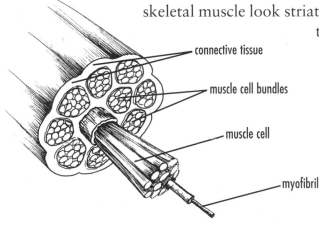

connective tissue

muscle cell bundles

muscle cell

myofibril

Muscles are bundles of muscle cells encased in connective tissue.

In the middle of the sarcomere, the A band is formed by myosin filaments and actin filaments that overlap them. In the I band, actin from two adjacent sarcomeres comes together at the Z line. Another protein, titin, stabilizes the thick filaments of myosin, connecting them to the Z line. Still other proteins, troponin and tropomyosin, wrap around actin, preventing myosin from interacting with actin when the muscle is not contracting.

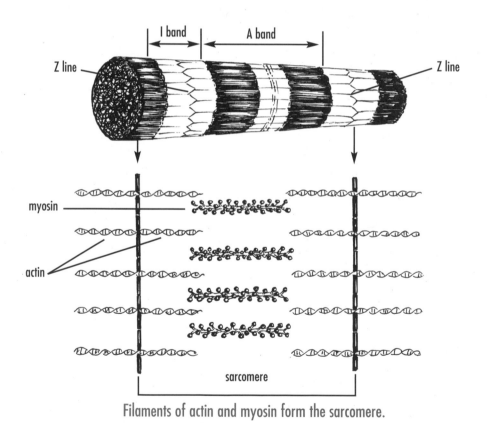

Filaments of actin and myosin form the sarcomere.

The plasma (outer) membrane of a muscle cell is called the sarcolemma. It's specialized to conduct a signal from a motor (motion-signaling) nerve. When a nerve signal, or impulse, arrives there, it triggers the release of calcium from storage sites inside the muscle fiber. The calcium ions (charged atoms) pull away the proteins troponin and tropomyosin that separate actin and myosin. That exposes receptor sites on actin. Receptor sites are places on molecules where other molecules can attach. Once exposed, each receptor can attach to one of myosin's club-like heads. That binding of myosin's head to a receptor site on the actin filament forms a crossbridge. The crossbridge is a temporary link between a thick and a thin filament.

The crossbridge is charged with energy. It pulls the actin filament of the I band into the A band. There it overlaps with myosin. Thus, the thin, actin filament slides past a thick, myosin filament. That drags the ends of the sarcomere toward the center, and the sarcomere gets shorter. After a short distance of sliding, the crossbridge detaches or breaks. Then the myosin head regains its former shape. It binds to a receptor site farther along the actin filament, and the process repeats. It continues as long as the muscle is active.

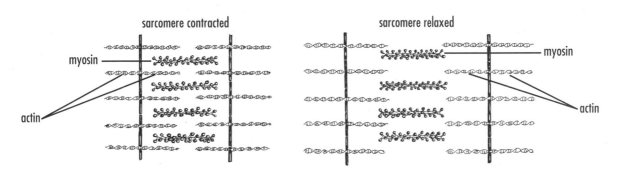

When a muscle contracts, myosin pulls the actin fibers closer together, shortening the sarcomere.

Zoologist Douglas Syme of the University of Calgary compares the process to a tug-of-war. "The filaments slide past one another as the thick filaments pull on the thin," he says, "much like the members of a tug-of-war team—the thick filaments—pulling on a rope—the thin filament. The hands of the team members repeatedly pull, let go, and grab on farther down the rope, pull again, and so on. All this pulling on the thin filaments causes the Z lines at the end of the sarcomere to draw closer together."[14] This process of forming, breaking, and repositioning crossbridges continues as long as the level of calcium ions remains high. When the level drops, the proteins that prevent actin and myosin from interacting return to their original positions, and the muscle relaxes.

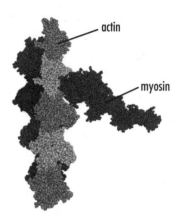

actin

myosin

In this space-filling model, actin is the long, thin gray molecule in the middle. The darker shape behind it is a second actin filament. The club-shaped molecule in the front is myosin. It is attaching to actin, forming a crossbridge.

What is a muscle cell's energy source?

The contraction of muscle requires an energy source. That source is ATP (adenosine triphosphate). (The *tri-* prefix means that three phosphate groups, written with the chemical symbols PO_4, are attached to the adenosine molecule.) The molecule stores a lot of energy in its phosphate bonds. When a bond breaks, energy is released. The energy is used to make the crossbridges that pull on the actin filament in the sarcomere. ADP (for adenosine diphosphate) is left over after one phosphate breaks away. (The *di-* prefix means that two phosphate groups are attached to the molecule.)

As much as muscle depends on ATP, it contains very little of it at any one time. In fact, a fast-running human would use up all the ATP in muscles in two to four seconds.[15] So, to keep going, the muscle must have a way to restore its ATP supply. The process of making ATP goes on in cellular structures called mitochondria. They are often called the "power plants" of the cell. They are always making fresh supplies of ATP. Mitochondria have not one way, but three, to get the job done. Two of the ways do not require oxygen (anaerobic). One does (aerobic).

First among the anaerobic sources is the molecule creatine phosphate. It traps and stores energy in its phosphate bonds just as ATP does. Creatine phosphate can "donate" phosphate groups to ADP when needed. The additional phosphate attaches to ADP, making a new ATP molecule. The cell's supply of creatine phosphate is limited. It's not even enough for 20 seconds of hard running.[16]

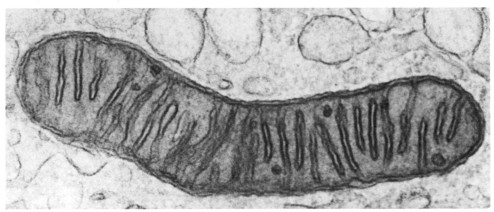

This image reveals the structure of a mitochondrion, where ATP is produced in a muscle cell.

This shortfall is overcome by another anaerobic process. It is glycolysis. The compound glycogen is stored in muscle. The mitochondria can break glycogen down into glucose. They then use that glucose to make ATP. No oxygen is used. The waste product of this process is lactic acid. Lactic acid causes the "burn" you feel during a sustained muscle contraction. When you feel the burn, the muscle is using anaerobic processes. During the recovery period, when muscle contraction stops, you breathe hard. You take in extra oxygen. This oxidizes the lactic acid and stops the burning. (You might think that lactic acid damages the muscle, but it doesn't. In fact, the acid shift affects the chemistry of muscle fibers so they stay "excitable," which lessens fatigue.[17])

The third source of energy for muscle is aerobic metabolism. Muscle fibers use glycogen from the liver and fat from the body's reserves to meet their energy needs. In a series of chemical reactions in mitochondria, oxygen is used to release energy from glucose (glycogen) and to transfer its energy to ATP. Since oxygen is present, lactic acid does not accumulate. Another form of aerobic metabolism is lipolysis, or the breakdown of fats to release energy. The chemical reactions that transfer fat's energy to ATP are a little different than for glucose, but the result is the same. The muscle cell has a plentiful and sustainable source of energy. Fat stored in muscles can provide up to 25 percent of the energy used by endurance athletes such as marathon runners.[18]

Are all muscle contractions the same?

No. A muscle has several different ways of generating force, and it does not always shorten. In an isometric contraction, for example, tension increases, but the muscle does not change its length and movement does not occur. An example of an isometric contraction is holding a heavy package in your arms. You don't move the package, but the force of the contracted muscles in your arms counteracts the force of gravity pulling down on the package.

Other contractions produce movement. They can be classified as concentric and eccentric. In a concentric contraction, the muscle tenses and shortens. An example is the lifting part of a bicep curl in which you raise your hand toward your shoulder while bending at the elbow. In an eccentric contraction, the muscle tenses and lengthens. Eccentric contractions usually occur when a muscle acts to oppose the force of gravity, such as during the lowering phase of a bicep curl.

Yet another type of muscle action is passive stretching. The muscle lengthens while it is relaxed. An example is the pull you feel behind your knees when you bend to touch your toes. The pull might feel like it's a whole muscle or bone action, but it actually occurs within the muscle cells themselves.

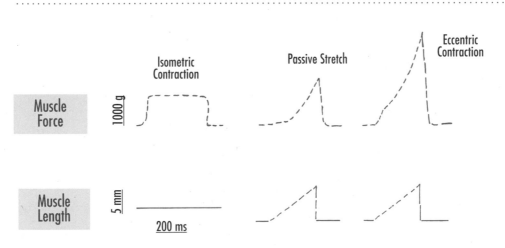

Muscle force varies with the type of contraction. A muscle need not shorten to exert a force.

Yes, although you probably don't notice the difference.

The response of a single muscle fiber to a single nerve impulse is called a twitch. Some muscle cells are slow twitch. Others are fast twitch. A twitch actually occurs in three phases:

- **The latent period,** about 2 milliseconds (0.002 seconds), is the time between the initiation of the activating nerve impulse and the generation of force.
- **The contraction period,** lasting from 10–100 milliseconds (0.001 to 0.1 seconds), is the time when force is increasing.
- **The relaxation period,** also lasting 10–100 milliseconds or longer, is the time when force is decreasing.[19]

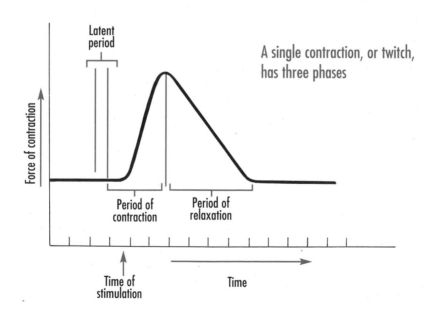

Latent period

A single contraction, or twitch, has three phases

Force of contraction

Period of contraction

Period of relaxation

Time of stimulation

Time

Redrawn from *Hole's Human Anatomy and Physiology*, 7th edition, by Shier, et al, copyright © 1996 TM Higher Education Group, Inc.

The speed of the twitch divides muscle cells into two main types: the red, which are called Type I fibers; and the white, which are called Type II fibers.

Type I fibers are slow twitch. They are red because they contain a lot of the red-pigmented molecule myoglobin. Myoglobin, like the red pigment hemoglobin in the blood, binds to oxygen, but it's an even better "grabber." It can pull oxygen out of the blood and move it into muscle. Myoglobin molecules act as a sort of "bucket brigade." Their action moves oxygen into muscle cells at a more rapid pace than simple diffusion would produce.[20] Slow-twitch fibers contain many mitochondria. They rely mostly on chemical reactions that use oxygen to make ATP. They are aerobic. Slow-twitch fibers dominate in muscles that must maintain contraction for long periods, such as the muscles that maintain upright posture. They also contribute to endurance and sustained performance in sports. Marathon runners may have as much as 80 percent slow-twitch fibers.

Type II fibers are fast twitch. They contain little myoglobin, so they are white. They also contain relatively few mitochondria. But they have a rich store of glycogen, from which ATP may be made without oxygen. Fast-twitch fibers produce brief bursts of power and speed. Sprinters may have as much as 80 percent Type II muscle fibers. Type II fibers also go to work when more power is required. Try to lift the heaviest weight you can, and your body will recruit your fast-twitch cells to do the job.

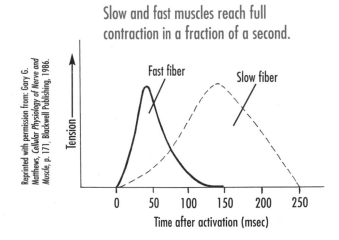

Slow and fast muscles reach full contraction in a fraction of a second.

Reprinted with permission from: Gary G. Matthews, *Cellular Physiology of Nerve and Muscle*, p. 171, Blackwell Publishing, 1986.

Normal muscle contractions are not a single twitch, but sustained contractions. The contraction can be sustained because nerves stimulate another twitch before the relaxation phase of the previous twitch can begin or be completed. That results in a continuing contraction of greater force. This is called a tetanus, or a tetanic contraction. Greater force also results from the recruitment of more muscle fibers to the task. That's why you can exert a small force to pet a puppy or a large one to lift a heavy box.

What are the fastest and slowest skeletal muscles?

Those of the eyes are fastest. They can contract in less then 1/100th of a second. The slowest is the soleus in the lower leg. It keeps the body upright by contracting in 1/10th of a second.[21]

How do nerves trigger the contractions of skeletal muscles?

In muscles, specialized nerve cells called motor neurons divide into tiny branches that send signals to individual muscle fibers. The nerve cells do not touch the muscle cells. Instead, their communication is chemical. When a nerve impulse arrives at the end of a motor neuron, chemical changes in the neuron trigger the release of the neurotransmitter acetylcholine. (Neurotransmitters are chemicals, often proteins, that carry messages between neurons or from neurons to other kinds of cells.) Acetylcholine crosses the gap between the neuron and the muscle fiber. On the muscle cell, it binds to specific receptor sites, where it fits like a key in a lock.

The binding launches the sequence of chemical and electrical events that leads to contraction. Chemical changes depend on the work of enzymes, which speed up reactions in cells. The enzyme acetylcholinesterase is an important enzyme. It breaks down the acetylcholine so it cannot continue to bind to the muscle membrane. This ensures that the muscle contracts only once in response to a single nerve impulse.

The site where a neuron and muscle meet is called the neuromuscular junction. The group of muscle cells that is triggered by a single motor neuron is a motor unit. All the fibers in a motor unit are of the same type (Type I or Type II), although a complete skeletal muscle contains a mixture of both types. The fibers in one motor unit contract simultaneously when triggered by an impulse from one motor neuron. A single motor unit may contain as few as 50 or as many as 400 muscle fibers.[22] An entire muscle may contain many hundreds of motor units. The gastrocnemius muscle of the calf, for example, contains more than 500.[23]

Do nerves cause cardiac and smooth muscle to contract?

Yes, but the mechanisms differ a little from those in skeletal muscles. Cardiac muscle cells contract on their own, without any stimulation from a nerve cell. Motor nerves do run to the heart, but they affect only the speed and strength of the heartbeat. Many smooth muscles, such as the ones in the stomach and intestines, don't need nerve stimulation to contract either. However, their action can be affected by motor nerves that stimulate or relax them, depending on which neurotransmitter they release at the neuromuscular junction. Smooth muscle may also contract in response to certain chemicals. For example, the hormone oxytocin stimulates contractions of the uterus during childbirth. Another example is an asthma attack. It is a series of contractions of the smooth muscle lining the air passages. It is triggered by histamine, which the immune system releases in response to a foreign substance, such as pollen or animal dander.

How much of human body weight is muscle?

On the average, muscles account for about 35 percent of a woman's body weight and 45 percent of a man's. (By comparison, bones account for only 12 percent.)[24] But that doesn't mean that more than one-third of your cells are muscle cells. Of your 100 trillion cells,[25] only about 0.0003 percent are skeletal muscle.[25] Cardiac and smooth muscle are an even smaller percentage.

How many muscles does a human have?

Estimates range from 640 to 700, with more than 50 in your face alone.[26] The number is not exact for several reasons:

- Experts disagree about whether some muscles are single muscles or two that are closely associated and working together.
- Males and females differ. For example, women have a uterus and men don't. Men have muscles that propel sperm and seminal fluid from the body during ejaculation, and women don't.
- Muscles differ among individuals. They can be duplicated, split, or absent. For example, a muscle in the lower arm called the palmaris longus is absent in about 14 percent of the population.[27]

This muscle flexes the hand—but so do some other muscles of the forearm, so it's never missed.

What are the largest and smallest human muscles?

The heaviest is the gluteus maximus of the buttocks.

The smallest one you can control is the levator palpebrae superioris. This tiny muscle raises the upper eyelid. The smallest one you can't control is the stapedius. It is in the middle ear. It is about 1/25th of an inch (1 millimeter) long. The stapedius moves the tiniest bone in the body—the stapes, or stirrup bone. The stirrup (along with the hammer and anvil bones) transmits sound vibrations through the middle ear. The stapedius does an important job. It clamps down on the ear bones during loud sounds so the bones don't vibrate too much. Its action protects the ear from damage, but it has its limits. Sustained loud sound, such as amplified music at a rock concert, damages the stapedius. Permanent hearing loss is the result.

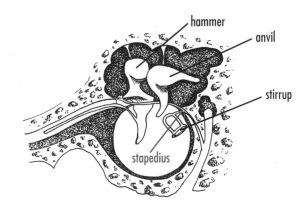

hammer

anvil

stirrup

stapedius

The smallest muscle in the body is involuntary. It moves a tiny bone in the middle ear.

What is muscle tone?

Tone is the natural stiffness or tension in a resting muscle. To a point, the greater a muscle's tone, the better it operates when it contracts. Good muscle tone improves coordination, balance, and joint function. The ideal value for muscle tone lies somewhere in the middle of a wide range of possible values. Too little is hypotonia. In infants, doctors may diagnose "floppy baby syndrome." This is not a disorder in itself but a symptom of some abnormality of the nervous system or muscles. Too much muscle tone is hypertonia. It occurs in people with cerebral palsy, Parkinson's disease, and other disorders.

How do muscles grow?

Muscle cells do not divide and reproduce. The number you are born with is the number you have throughout life. Overall muscle size increases because cells get larger—not more numerous—as a result of growth or exercise.

Muscle cells can, however, be replaced if they die as a result of injury or other damage. Here's what happens: Specialized satellite cells lie just above active muscle fibers. Normally they are dormant. When hormones stimulate muscle cell replacement, muscle fibers use the gas nitric oxide to "turn on" satellite cells.[28] Then the satellite cells begin to multiply and develop into muscle cells. They eventually fuse with existing fibers. It might seem that this process would eventually deplete the muscle of satellite cells, but that is not the case. When satellite cells divide, some of their "daughter" cells remain undifferentiated (unspecialized) as new satellite cells.

Why don't muscles get ridiculously huge?

Muscle tissue self-regulates. It produces a protein called myostatin, which slows muscle growth. The bigger a muscle gets, the more myostatin it produces. When the level of myostatin reaches a certain threshold value, it causes muscle growth to cease. It works by blocking the activation of satellite cells.

Research on myostatin is more than an intellectual exercise for scientists. They hope to find ways to block its action in treating muscle-wasting diseases such as muscular dystrophy (see Chapter 4). In one study, scientists worked with a molecule called ACVR2B. It binds to myostatin, blocking its action. In lab mice, it causes skeletal muscle to get bulkier.[29]

What is the strongest muscle?

The answer depends on how you define strength. It might mean force. In physics, a force is a push or a pull that changes the velocity of an object. Using that definition, the strongest muscles are those with the largest cross-sectional area. They are the gluteus maximus of the buttocks and the big muscles of the thighs. For example, the hamstring muscles in the backs of the thighs of healthy young men can exert 1,000 pounds (4,500 newtons) of force.[30]

But strength can be defined in another way—as power. Power is the amount of work a muscle does in a given amount of time. Two muscles may exert the same force, but if one works at a faster rate, its power is greater. The unit of power is the watt. "For ordinary skeletal muscles, power output pretty well follows weight," says biologist

Steven Vogel. "If [a muscle is] the heaviest, then it's the most powerful."[31] Power calculations show that a heavy muscle such as the quadriceps in the thigh can achieve a power output of around 100 watts. In comparison, the power output of a healthy human heart is at best—during strenuous exercise—only about 5 watts.[32]

How efficient are muscles?

Efficiency is the ratio of work output to work input. Physicists define work as a force applied across a distance. Work is often measured in a unit called a joule. You do a certain number of joules of work when you work against gravity to lift a box from the floor. The heavier the box and the farther you lift it, the greater the number of joules of work you do.

No machine—either natural or human-made—is 100 percent efficient. Some energy is always lost to the environment as heat. For example, consider a cyclist who performs 100,000 joules of work while pedaling a bicycle uphill. Only 60,000 joules actually do the work of getting the cyclist and the bike to the top. The rest is lost as heat. In this example, the cyclist and the bike are 60 percent (60,000/100,000) efficient.

Scientists measure the oxygen consumption of subjects pedaling exercise bikes to calculate the efficiency of muscle. They find that, for every milliliter of oxygen used, about 20 joules of food energy are released, but only about 5 joules of useful work are done in moving the pedals. Thus, the efficiency of muscles is about 5/20 or 25 percent under laboratory conditions. In real life, efficiency runs closer to 20 percent.[33]

How do
muscles develop
before birth?

In the early cell divisions that follow union of human egg and sperm, all cells are the same. They form a hollow ball of cells that haven't yet developed specialized functions. That situation does not last long. In the fifth week of pregnancy, an important process occurs. It is gastrulation. Gastrulation is the movement of cell layers into the interior of the ball. It's a complicated process, but the result is three layers of cells that will develop into different kinds of tissues and organs. The outer layer becomes skin and nerves. The inner layer develops into the internal organs. The middle layer, or mesoderm, will form bones and muscles.

Soon the mesodermal layer thickens. It forms somites on both sides of the notochord (where the backbone will develop later). As time goes on, the somites will become arms and legs. The part of the somite that lies toward the back of the embryo will become the muscles of the chest and abdomen. From that region also grow satellite cells. These eventually become muscle cells.[34]

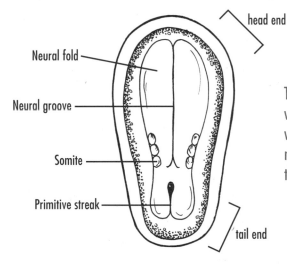

The human embryo in the fifth week of pregnancy. The somites will become arms and legs. The neural groove will develop into the spinal cord.

A cell destined to become a skeletal muscle cell is called a myoblast. At certain times, inhibitory proteins block the action of enzymes that make myoblasts reproduce themselves. When that happens, myoblasts begin to develop into true muscle fibers.[35] Where muscles will form in the somites, myoblasts line up side-by-side with connective tissue, which forms where bone and cartilage are growing. Several myoblasts fuse to become a myotube, which is a hollow cylinder of myofibrils. Each myotube then develops further into a functioning muscle cell, the mature fiber. The fusion of many myoblasts—each with its own nucleus—is the reason skeletal muscle cells have many nuclei.

Communication between motor nerves and motor units must be established at the neuromuscular junction. The proper nerve ending must grow in the right direction and end up at the right muscle. The nerve, it seems, needs a "road map" to follow. The muscle cells themselves provide at least part of that road map. As the embryo develops, each muscle cell has along its length many sites where such link-ups might form. But within a few weeks, all the potential sites disappear except for those that come close to a motor neuron that is growing toward them from the spinal cord. How does this happen? Muscle cells make proteins that guide nerves toward the middle of the muscle band.[36] They make precise amounts of proteins called ephrins that "point the way."[37]

Later, the neurons themselves control which sites develop as neuromuscular junctions. As they grow toward the muscle cells, they release a protein called agrin and the neurotransmitter acetylcholine. Acetylcholine prevents a neuromuscular junction from forming at many of the possible sites on the muscle fiber. However, where the end of the nerve comes close to a muscle cell, agrin is concentrated enough to overcome acetylcholine's negative effect. As a result, a neuromuscular junction forms at the end of the neuron at the precise point where it comes closest to the muscle fiber.[38]

As all this is happening internally, external changes are occurring too. Toward the end of the fifth week of development, the upper and lower jawbones and muscles begin to develop. In the seventh week, the upper limb buds are paddle-shaped. The lower limb buds look like flippers. The shape of thigh, calf, and foot begin to appear in the leg limb buds. In the eighth week, fingers begin forming. It's another week before toes appear. The embryo moves, twitching its body and limb buds.

At ten weeks, the embryo measures 1 inch (2.5 cm) long. It is now called a fetus. At this time, bones begin to harden in the leg. This is an important milestone, because the growth of muscles and tendons depends on bone growth. Lewis Wolpert explains:

> The coordination of the growth is achieved mainly by mechanical means; the growing bones pull on muscles and tendons making them grow. It seems that the stimulus to the growth in length of muscles and tendons is just tension—pull. If, for example, the growth of a bone is delayed, so too will be that of the associated muscles and tendons. In this way, the lengths of muscles, tendons, and bones are nicely adjusted to each other.[39]

If all goes well, this process of interactive growth continues for an additional 26 weeks or so. It produces a newborn that, at (usually) 6 to 9 pounds (2.7–4.1 kilograms) in weight, is about 20 percent muscle.[40]

Muscling around the Animal Kingdom[41]

. . . . .

If I were as strong as the ant, proportionally, I could throw grand pianos, carry drums of oil in either hand, lift cars out of their parking spaces, uproot respectable trees, and pick up between 1,500 and 2,000 pounds of whole wheat bread. I would be a comic book hero who didn't need a car jack, a forklift, or a moving van.[42]

—JAN ADKINS, *MOVING HEAVY THINGS*

. . . . .

Some people say you are what you eat, but what you *do* is a matter for the muscles. "The most important effectors for animal behavior are the muscles," say zoologists Douglas Syme and Robert Josephson.[43] The things animals can do are mostly determined "by the ability of muscles to produce force and to do work, the speed of their responses, [and] their efficiency in converting chemical to mechanical energy."[44] If that all sounds a lot like chemistry and physics to you, you have the right idea. How animals achieve quick responses and sus-tained action depends on the structure and function of their muscles. The sloth, for example, is a slow-moving animal because its muscles are incapable of a rapid response. In contrast, a mosquito can fly because its wings can move back and forth at a frequency ten times what human muscles can achieve.

Whether muscles are fast twitch or slow twitch, however, has little to do with how quickly they shorten. What differs is the power that the muscle produces. Power is the speed of shortening multiplied by the force that is generated. Fast-twitch muscles produce a large force while they contract, so they deliver more power than slow muscles can. "Think of you versus a bulldozer," Syme explains. "You are a slow muscle and a bulldozer is a fast muscle. The bulldozer is capable of moving a little faster than you move if it is pushed to its limit (which is why it is called 'fast' and you are 'slow'), but that in itself is not so important. You are quite capable of moving just as fast as a bulldozer as it pushes piles of dirt around (when it is doing something useful), so being able to shorten fast is not the important characteristic of being a fast muscle. What is important is that the bulldozer can generate a lot of force as it is moving around, whereas you (the slow muscle) are not capable of generating that much force.

"The bulldozer can generate a lot more power than you, and that makes it useful. (Not implying that you are not useful!) For several reasons you (the slow muscle) would be much better for doing tasks that don't require so much power. Bulldozers aren't good at making toast or writing letters or doing heart surgery, nor are they particularly fuel efficient. My point is that fast muscles are indeed fast, but for most activities, it isn't the speed itself that is important. What's important is that fast muscles can maintain high force when they shorten (they are powerful), and that is what makes them good for activities like sprinting and weightlifting."[45]

Fast, powerful muscles work because the crossbridges that form between actin and myosin cycle rapidly, as does the movement of calcium. Syme compares these muscles to a souped-up engine. "It's like putting a four-barrel carburetor and

The mantis shrimp is the fastest puncher in the animal world. It can jab at over 50 miles (80 km) per hour.

Black bears lose little of their muscle strength during hibernation. Some scientists think massive bouts of shivering provide the exercise needed to keep muscles strong.

overboring the cylinders on an engine; it's the same engine, just modified for high speed or high power," he says. Just as a high-performance engine requires a lot of energy, so do contractions of fast muscles. They use a lot of ATP.

Fast muscles are also needed to power activities in animals that require rapid, regular fluctuations in force, such as the flapping wings in a hummingbird's flight or producing vibrations for sound. The cicada, for example, vibrates its tymbals (round plates on its abdomen) to make a buzzing sound. Contraction of the tymbal muscles swings the tymbals inward. This buckles the ribs of the cicada's tymbals one at a time, causing each of them to twist into a V-shape. The result? A series of clicks that resonate through an air sac in the cicada's abdomen. It works much like an empty soda can that clicks inward when you squeeze it. The clicks are rapid because the fast tymbal muscle contracts, recovers, and contracts again at a high frequency.[46]

Producing a sound like the cicada's requires more than powerful, high-frequency movements. The muscles must move in synchrony (at the same time). They can do that because they are stimulated by coordinated nerve impulses. The cells in the tymbal muscles all belong to a single motor unit. They are activated together. For each nerve impulse, there is a single muscle contraction.

Not all animal muscles work that way. Some are asynchronous; they don't move at the same time. In asynchronous muscles, one nerve activation generally results in several cycles of muscle contraction and relaxation. So a contraction need not be triggered by a nerve impulse. Most flying insects stay airborne because of the asynchronous muscles of their wings. A nerve impulse "turns on" a wing muscle, but once it's activated, the muscle continues to contract and relax as long as it is bearing a load. The load is the wing of the insect. Only occasional nerve activation is required to keep the muscles contracting.

Evolutionary biologists think asynchronous muscles evolved from the synchronous kind. "For high-frequency operation they are both more powerful and more efficient than their synchronous counterparts," say Syme and Josephson.[47] They think asynchronous muscles are one big reason why insects are such successful life forms. "The insects have produced the jet engine of the animal world," Syme says. "They still use calcium to turn the muscle on and off, and they still use thick and thin filaments and crossbridges, but they have tweaked the rules by which the filaments interact and how the nerves control the muscle, allowing them to pack a lot more power into the same mass of muscle."[48]

CHAPTER TWO

QUESTIONS

ABOUT SPECIFIC MUSCLES

Nothing is more revealing than movement.[49]
—MARTHA GRAHAM,
NAMED BY *TIME* MAGAZINE AS THE "DANCER OF THE [20TH] CENTURY"

Why do muscles have such long names, and what do they mean?

Anatomy is an old science. It dates back to the ancient Greeks and Romans who gave bones, muscles, and joints descriptive names that were easy to remember—for them! To English speakers, the names seem long and difficult, but there are patterns to them. Once you get the hang of the logic, the names aren't so hard. In fact, the names often describe the size, location, or function of the muscle.

Many of the muscle names identify the two points they connect. For example, the sternocleidomastoid muscle attaches the sternum (breastbone) and clavicle (collarbone) to the mastoid process of the

• 44 •

temporal bone, which lies in the head, behind the ear. So the name tells you the origin and insertion of the muscle.

Many other muscle names come from Latin and Greek words that describe what the muscle looks like. For example, the transversus abdominis comes from Latin and means "across the belly," which is exactly where the muscle lies. Two other abdominal muscles are the internal and external obliques. Oblique means diagonal, which is the direction in which those muscles run. Some names are almost poetic. The gracilis muscle gets its name from the Latin word for slender and graceful. It is just that—a long, slim muscle. It runs from the lower edge of the pubic bone to the lower leg, behind the knee. Make a side kick—gracefully, please!—and you are using it.

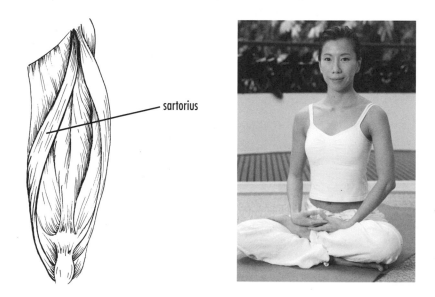

sartorius

The sartorius is a long muscle of the thigh. Sartorius means "tailor" in Latin. The contraction of the sartorius pulls the legs into the cross-legged sitting position of a traditional tailor.

What muscles are
used in eating?

Nearly all the muscles of the head and neck get into the act when we bite, chew, and swallow food. The muscles of the lips, jaw, tongue, hard and soft palate (inside the mouth), cheeks, and throat produce a complex, coordinated series of movements.

Five pairs of muscles connect the lower jaw to the skull. Three of them close the jaw and produce three actions: shutting, clamping down, and grinding:

- The temporalis muscle shuts the mouth. It is a powerful muscle. Its origin is at the temple and its insertion is at the upper jawbone.
- The masseter muscle raises the lower jaw and clamps the mouth shut. It originates on the cheekbone and inserts into the bottom of the jaw.
- The lateral and medial pterygoid muscles alternate their contractions to produce a grinding motion of the jaw. They arise from the cheekbone and palate areas of the skull. They insert into the back parts of the jawbone.

Three major muscles let you chew your food.

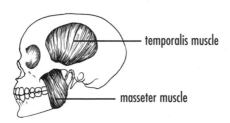

temporalis muscle

masseter muscle

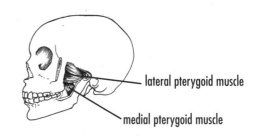

lateral pterygoid muscle

medial pterygoid muscle

During chewing, the lower jaw moves up and down and from side to side in an elliptical path. It crushes and grinds food. Although you chew on only one side at a time, you use the jaw-closing muscles on both sides.[50] To prove that to yourself, chew some gum on one side while putting your fingers at your jaw joint—just below and in front of your ear—on the other side. You'll feel the masseter muscle working.

Muscles in the cheeks and tongue hold food between the teeth for chewing. The genioglossus muscle under the tongue both depresses the tongue and thrusts it forward. The tongue itself is not one muscle, but eight.[51] In it, muscle fibers are arranged in layers. They run in many different directions—horizontally, vertically, and diagonally. They make it possible to flex and extend the tongue, manipulate its tip, and roll the tongue around. In the throat, the tongue connects to the U-shaped hyoid bone, which is sometimes called the tongue bone. Four muscles attached there support and move the tongue up, down, and from side to side.

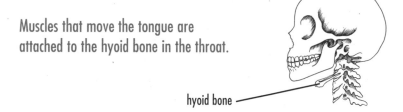

Muscles that move the tongue are attached to the hyoid bone in the throat.

hyoid bone

The tongue moves food in the mouth. It rises to push food back toward the throat. Muscles in the palate rise, letting food pass back through the mouth. Then they automatically contract to force food down into the throat for swallowing. Even the muscles of the larynx, or voice box, are part of the process. They rise to allow food to enter the esophagus. Then they drop during swallowing.

The first action is the tongue pushing food back into the throat. The throat rises and expands to accept it. To block food from going into the nose, the soft palate at the back of the mouth closes off the nasal passage. The epiglottis blocks the windpipe to the lungs and closes over the vocal cords. These actions prevent food from getting into the airways. They are the reason you can't breathe or talk while swallowing.

The soft palate and epiglottis block the airways during swallowing.

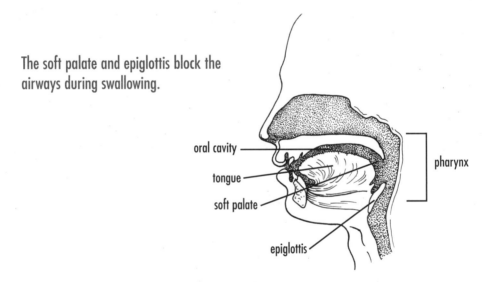

oral cavity

tongue

soft palate

epiglottis

pharynx

In a normal swallow, a ring of muscle called the upper esophageal sphincter opens. It allows food to move from the throat into the esophagus. It closes and a wave of smooth muscle contraction pushes the food toward the stomach. If you are seated or standing, gravity helps move the food along, although gravity is not necessary to move food into your stomach. It's possible to eat or drink while standing on your head.

Anything that harms the muscles or nerves of the throat or esophagus can cause dysphagia. Dysphagia is difficulty swallowing. It's fairly common. It affects one in every ten people over the age of fifty.[52] It can be treated with medication, changes in diet, exercises that make the swallowing muscles stronger, or surgery that stretches the esophagus.

Another sphincter operates at the junction where the esophagus meets the stomach. It is called the lower esophageal (or cardiac) sphincter. It opens to allow food to move into the stomach. When you are not swallowing, both the upper and lower sphincters normally remain closed. That prevents food and stomach acid from moving backward—from the stomach into the esophagus or from the esophagus into the mouth. Gastroesophageal reflux, also known as acid reflux or heartburn, is a backflow of stomach acid upward into the esophagus through the lower esophageal sphincter.

How do the muscles of the digestive tract work?

Peristalsis is the automatic, involuntary, slow contraction of the organs of the digestive tract. It begins in the esophagus and continues through the stomach into the small and large intestines. It works because muscle fibers surround the outside of the tube that is the digestive tract. When they contract, they decrease the diameter of the tube, pushing food and wastes ahead of the contraction.

With a stethoscope, you can hear the contractions in the small intestine. Sometimes, when it is moving long and hard, you can hear its rumbles and squeals without assistance. These noises are the result of nerve action. Nerves in the gut release the neurotransmitter acetylcholine. It speeds peristalsis.

Peristalsis assists in defecation (elimination of solid waste), but the abdominal muscles play a part too. They create pressure in the body cavity that helps push feces out. After defecation, the coccygeus muscle pulls the coccyx (the lower tip of the backbone) forward and assists in closing the outlet. When defecation is not occurring, the anus is sealed by an inner ring of smooth muscle and an outer ring of striated muscle. They contract and seal to prevent leakage. Blood-filled, spongy pads of tissue inside the inner ring assist them. These are called hemorrhoids. They are a normal part of the body. They are not a disorder, as ads for potions designed to shrink them imply. They require treatment only when they bulge outside the anus and cause itching or pain.

Do I use muscles when I vomit?

Yes, but vomiting is not reverse peristalsis. (See previous question.) When you vomit, the muscles of the stomach and esophagus relax. The cardiac sphincter, which normally closes between the base of the esophagus and the top of the stomach, remains open. Then the abdominal muscles and diaphragm contract strongly, pushing against the stomach. The result is a powerful spasm that propels stomach contents up and out. Between the stomach and the upper part of the small intestine lies a ring of smooth muscle called the pyloric sphincter. If it opens, material from the small intestine may also be expelled.

What muscles control breathing?

When you inhale, muscles contract to make the sternum move upward and the ribs rise. The pectoralis minor in the chest pulls up on the rib cage. At the same time, contraction of the diaphragm, which is the main muscle of breathing, causes it to drop and flatten. These movements increase the volume of the space inside the chest, where the lungs are. Here, some basic physics goes to work. In the increased space inside, air pressure is less than on the outside of the body. As a result, air moves into the lungs. That inhalation equalizes the pressure. When the diaphragm relaxes, it rises, and the muscles that move the ribs and sternum relax. The pressure is greater inside than out, so you push air out, or exhale.

When you hold your breath, you keep the muscles of your diaphragm contracted so it's down. When you push out as much air as you can, you let your relaxed diaphragm rise into its highest position. You may also call upon the quadratus lumborum, a muscle in the low back, to pull down hard on your bottom ribs. (People sometimes strain that muscle when they sneeze too hard.) When you force a deep inhalation, you bring other muscles into the act, including the external intercostals and the scalene muscles. The intercostals lie between the ribs. The scalenes are attached to the vertebrae of the neck. They normally support the upper ribs.

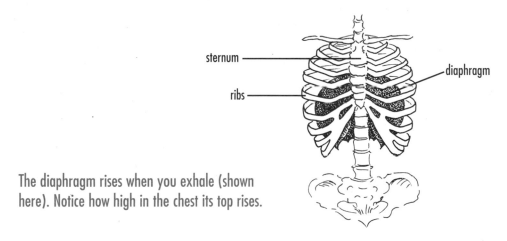

sternum

ribs

diaphragm

The diaphragm rises when you exhale (shown here). Notice how high in the chest its top rises.

The diaphragm has another job to do. Its alternating pattern of contraction and relaxation changes pressure inside the body cavity. That rhythm helps return blood and lymph to the heart.[53] The Heimlich maneuver is one form of first aid for people who are choking. It works because pressure on the diaphragm increases pressure in the chest cavity, forcing blocked food up and out of the windpipe.

What muscles produce speech and singing?

The sounds of speech and singing come from the larynx. It's in the throat, above the windpipe. Muscles attach the larynx to the hyoid bone of the throat, the sternum, and the soft tissues of the throat and esophagus.

The larynx is a box that can vibrate. It is made of three plates of cartilage that house and support a pair of muscular membranes called the vocal folds. When a brain decides that its owner should comment on the weather or sing an aria, nerve impulses travel from the brain to the larynx. The impulses trigger contraction of muscles that pull on the cartilage plates and change the shape of the vocal folds. Also, the muscles of the vocal folds themselves can tighten and flex in different ways. When air passes through contracted vocal folds, they vibrate, and a sound is made. The volume, pitch, and tone of the sound depend on how the vocal folds tense and stretch—and in what direction—thereby changing their rate of vibration. When the folds relax, exhaled air passes unhindered through the larynx and no sound is made.

The muscles of the tongue play a big part in shaping sounds from the larynx into recognizable words. The tongue subtly changes its shape with every vowel and consonant. Tongue muscles are compartmentalized. They are made up of smaller, individual segments that can be controlled independently. The tongue can activate localized areas along its length with extremely fine control. Some evidence suggests that slow-twitch muscle fibers in the tongue deliver this precise control. The adult human tongue is 54 percent slow-twitch fibers. In newborns, it's only 31 percent. That suggests that the development of speech and the development of slow-twitch muscle fibers in the tongue go hand-in-hand.[54]

What muscles keep me upright?

Nearly all the muscles of the body get involved, but the two deepest of the back's five muscle layers do most of the work.[55] The deepest layer of the back muscles supports the vertebrae. A row of these muscles runs from the upper vertebrae of the neck to the lowest vertebrae at the coccyx. Some of these small muscles work in the space between two vertebrae. Others overlap more than two, and many hook to the ribs. These muscles help you bend your back or turn your body, but they are working even when you are not moving. They are active at all times. They maintain the length of the backbone whether you are standing or lying down. How do they do this without getting tired? These deep muscles alternate contraction and relaxation up and down the back. When some are contracting, others get a rest.

The next layer is important for posture too. To feel it, lie on your back with your knees up and bent. Then stretch and elongate your spine. (This should feel very good!) What you are feeling is the relaxation of the extensor muscles that run the length of the spine in three columns of overlapping bundles. Their stable attachment is the sacrum, a bone at the base of the spine. They rise from there in sections that connect to the ribs, upper back, neck, and head. When you stand, they oppose the forward pull of the weight in your arms, chest, belly, and hips. You'd fall on your nose if this second layer of deep back muscle wasn't constantly pulling you back and up, keeping you (more or less) vertical.

What muscles support the internal organs?

The lungs, heart, and stomach are encased inside the bony cage of the sternum and the ribs, but the organs below that have no skeletal support. Membranes called mesenteries attach to the abdominal cavity at the back. They support and stabilize the intestines. Mesenteries also contain the blood vessels, nerves, and lymph vessels that supply the cells of the intestine with food and oxygen. Mesenteries are not muscles, however. They are flexible and provide little support compared to the muscles that surround the abdomen.

Bands of muscles run vertically, horizontally, and diagonally to encase and protect the entire area. Several of them are continuous with the muscles of the rib cage. (That's why you feel tension in your abdominal muscles when you lie on your back and lift your chest off the floor.) Four major abdominal muscles are as follows:

- The rectus abdominis is the vertical muscle that forms the muscular bumps that can be seen on the bellies of bodybuilders. (It's the only one you can see externally. The others are flat sheets.) Its origin is at the pubic bone. It runs upward to attach to several ribs. This muscle is a powerful flexor. You use it whenever you sit up. Working in opposition to the extensor muscles of the back, it helps in walking and standing upright. Bodybuilders should note that "six-pack abs" is a misnomer. The muscle actually has four "bellies" on each side, for a total of eight.

- The external oblique is the outer layer of the side muscles of the abdomen. It runs from the lowest ribs downward and attaches to the top of the pelvic bone. A tough, flat sheet of connective tissue also attaches it to the middle-front of the body. You use it when you twist your body from side to side.

- The internal oblique is the middle layer. It has its origin on the pelvic bone and the connective tissue of the lower backbone. It fans out to attach to the ribs, the pubic bone, and the middle-front. You use it when you cough, sneeze, or exhale with force.

- The transversus abdominis (or transversalis) is the innermost layer. It runs horizontally around the midriff. It is attached to several bones with several sheets of connective tissue. "Suck in your gut" and you'll feel your transversalis.

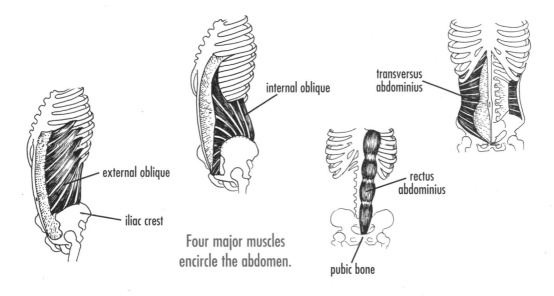

internal oblique

transversus abdominius

external oblique

iliac crest

rectus abdominius

pubic bone

Four major muscles encircle the abdomen.

What muscles
control urination?

The kidneys manufacture urine. It travels though tubes called ureters to the bladder. There it is stored. The bladder muscle stretches as it fills, up to a maximum volume of about 2 cups (500 milliliters) in adults. You feel the need to urinate when pressure on your bladder sends signals to your brain. The fuller your bladder, the greater your perceived need to urinate.

Elimination of urine begins with a signal sent from the brain to the muscular walls of the bladder. The signal stimulates the bladder to contract. This forces urine into a tube called the urethra. The urethra opens to the outside of the body. Most of the time, the sphincter muscles of the urethra are contracted, keeping the tube closed. But when urination begins, nerve signals from the brain cause them to relax. As the bladder contracts, so do the muscles of the abdominal wall. They increase pressure on the bladder and aid in forcing urine down and out from the urethra. During urination, the bladder and the muscles of the abdomen may alternately contract and relax several times. Muscles of the pelvic floor, which run between the pubic bone in the front and the tip of the backbone in the rear, support the urethra and bladder. Squeezing and relaxing them stops and starts the stream of urine.

What muscles
are used in
walking?

It takes 11 joints and 57 muscles to perform the deceptively simple act of walking.[56] As you step forward, your pelvis shifts, the muscles of your buttocks contract, and the front leg pulls you forward. At the same time, your back leg pushes, using muscles that flex the foot and the big toe. Muscles of the abdomen, back, and chest hold the body erect and shift to maintain balance. Your hips move forward, backward, and side-to-side. The lower and side abdominal muscles contract and relax. The arms usually get into the act too. You swing them when strolling or pump them when power walking.

Three major muscle groups contract across the hip, down the thigh, and over the knee to produce the large leg movements of walking. The muscles act on both the hip and knee joints at once, so the action is smooth and rhythmic. They are the

- muscles of the inner thigh, which extend and flex the knee and stabilize the leg when weight is on it;
- quadriceps, a group of several muscles in the thigh that extend both the knee and the upper leg at the hip;
- hamstrings, at the back of the leg, which extend the leg at the hip and (along with the calf muscles) extend the lower leg at the knee.

What muscles move the hand?

The hand is an engineering wonder. It is capable of gross movements, such as forming a fist, and fine movements, such as playing the piano. It achieves these feats through the action of some 29 to 38 muscles (depending on how you count them).[57]

Some of the muscles are in the hand, but many are in the lower arm. They move the hand because of tendons that run from the forearm to attachment points on the fingers. This arrangement has benefits. If all the muscles that move the hand were in the hand itself, the hand would be too bulky to perform fine movements.

The muscles of the hand and arm spread and close the fingers and lift and lower the thumb. The opposable thumb is one of the main reasons why humans are skilled makers and users of tools. Try this: While looking at your palm, bring your thumb and little finger together. Watch the bulge in the fleshy part of your palm, just below the thumb. When you see its bulge, you are actually seeing three muscles:

- Abductor pollicis brevis raises the thumb upwards;
- Flexor pollicis brevis flexes the thumb, curling it toward the palm;
- Opponens pollicis brings the thumb to the finger.

A fourth muscle involved in this action is the adductor pollicis. It begins at the bones in the middle of the palm and attaches higher on the thumb than the other three, so you don't see its contraction.

The muscles that make a fist are located not in the hand but in the lower arm. Tendons that run along the underside of the wrist bend the fingers toward the palm. Try this: Make a tight fist and bend your hand toward your arm. Look at the underside of your wrist. You'll see a tendon bulging there. It is actually part of a muscle that contracts higher on the arm, near the elbow. The same principle applies when you lift and lower your little finger. The muscle that performs that action, the extensor digiti minimi, starts on one of the bones of the forearm and attaches at the base the finger. Watch the back of your hand as you bend and flex your little finger. You'll see movement of a tendon at the knuckle.

What muscles produce facial expressions?

It takes 17 muscles to smile, but a frown requires 43. That's only the beginning of the range of emotions that facial expressions reveal. Facial expressions account for two-thirds of our nonverbal communications with others.[58] They fall into seven major categories that people in all cultures easily recognize: sadness, surprise, anger, contempt, disgust, fear, and happiness. More complex emotions such as relief, guilt, shame, or contentment are harder to "read." About 10,000 facial movements express emotions. (There's a computer at the Department of Defense that can read them all!)[59]

Expressions derive from combinations of muscle actions. The occipital frontalis muscle raises the eyebrows when you're surprised. The levator palpebrae superioris raises the upper eyelid when you're excited. The corrugator muscle lies between the eyebrows. It's the main frowning muscle. It produces vertical lines between the eyes. The procerus produces wrinkles over the bridge of your nose. You use it when you frown or when you're puzzled.

The lips play a role in many expressions. The levator labii superioris raises your upper lip in a snarl. The depressor anguli oris draws the angle of the mouth down and to the side, showing disapproval or producing a grimace. Want to pout? Use your depressor labii inferioris to drop your lower lip and your mentalis to wrinkle your chin. Clench your mouth in a tense line, and you are using your risorious muscle.

Elvis Presley's famous lip curl uses the muscle with the longest name: levator labii superioris alaeque nasi.

You use your zygomatic major when you smile. It originates in the cheekbone and inserts near the corner of the mouth. It lifts the corner of the mouth up and to the sides. But using it alone leads to a less-than-convincing smile. A more genuine smile involves the orbicularis oculi muscles that surround the eyes. There's another important muscle in the face. It's the orbicularis oris. It surrounds the mouth. It's an important one among the 34 you use for kissing.[60]

What muscles move the eye?

Roll your eyes and you use four muscles attached at the top, bottom, and sides of the eyeball. The superior rectus moves the eyeball skyward. The inferior rectus lets you look at the floor without moving your head. The lateral rectus and medial rectus move the eyes from side to side so you can watch a tennis match, again without moving your head.

Connective tissue maintains the shape of the eye as it rests in its bony socket. Focusing an image depends, in part, on the muscles of the eye. They move the eye and make fine adjustments to its shape, changing the focal length. These muscles move about 200,000 times a day.[61] Also important are the ciliary muscles in the eye that attach to the lens. They change its shape and focus the image on the retina at the back of the eye.

The medical term for eyelids is palpebrae. They are folds of skin and muscle lined with a membrane. Their muscle action covers or exposes the eyeball. The upper lid moves more than the lower. Eyelids protect the eye and reduce light input when we sleep. They protect against damage from bright lights and foreign objects. Their secretions keep the eyeball moist. Without your eyelid, you could not palpebrate, which means wink.[62]

Your ability to see also depends on muscles that dilate and constrict the pupil (the opening into the eye). Sphincter and dilator muscles in the iris (the colored part) respond to changing light levels. They enlarge the pupil when light is dim. They diminish its size in bright light. They respond to emotions in the same way. Fear, interest, and excitement enlarge the pupils no matter what the light level.

What causes a reflex?

Tap just below your knee and your lower leg will jerk. That's a reflex, and it's not under your control. A nerve pathway that runs from the quadriceps muscle of the thigh through your spinal cord and back to your quadriceps—without asking the brain's permission!—triggers it. Here's what happens:

- The tap pulls the kneecap down and stretches the quadriceps muscles in the thigh.
- The stretch initiates an impulse in sensory neurons. They send a signal to the spinal cord. There a response signal is initiated in a motor neuron.
- The motor signal travels back to the quadriceps muscles, causing them to contract. This action pulls the lower leg upward.

As simple as this sequence seems, it raises some puzzling questions. One is why the reflex stops with a single jerk. Remember that muscles work in opposing pairs. Contracting the quadriceps on the front of the knee stretches muscles in the back of the knee. That should, you might guess, elicit a contraction response in those muscles, prompting the knee to swing back and forth until exhaustion. But it does not, because

RICHMOND HEIGHTS

sensory neurons from the quadriceps form many branches in the spinal cord. Some of the branches send a signal that excites the quadriceps into contraction. Other branches communicate with different motor neurons that send "stop" messages to the muscles behind the knee.[63]

What controls the heart muscle?

Cardiac muscle cells will contract and relax spontaneously, even if removed from the body. They are arranged so that one cell stimulates its neighboring cells to contract. Natural contractions tend to be slower than the normal heartbeat, however, so other control mechanisms must be at work.

An electrical stimulus coordinates the rhythmic contraction of the heart's four chambers. The stimulus begins in the sinoatrial (SA) node in the right upper chamber (right atrium) of the heart. The impulse does not come from a nerve. A small group of specialized cells in the SA node generates it. The impulse sweeps across the muscle of the right and left atria. It causes them to contract and squeeze blood into the lower chambers, the ventricles, although not at the same time. That's because the electrical impulse first travels to the atrioventricular (AV) node, where a slight time delay is introduced. This delay allows the atria to empty before the ventricles begin to contract. The delay prevents back pressure and back flow. The AV node stimulates a specialized group of muscle cells called the bundle of His. (It is named for the German physician Wilhelm His Jr., who discovered it in 1893.) Protected by an outer sheath of connective tissue, the bundle runs from the right atrium down into the wall between the ventricles. There it divides into two bundles. They branch and provide a contractile impulse to both ventricles.

The SA node is muscle, but many nerves run to it. Nerves from the body's stress response system stimulate the SA node chemically and speed the heart rate. Nerves associated with the body's relaxation response slow the SA rhythm. These opposing systems let the body adjust the heart's speed to meet its changing needs for oxygen.

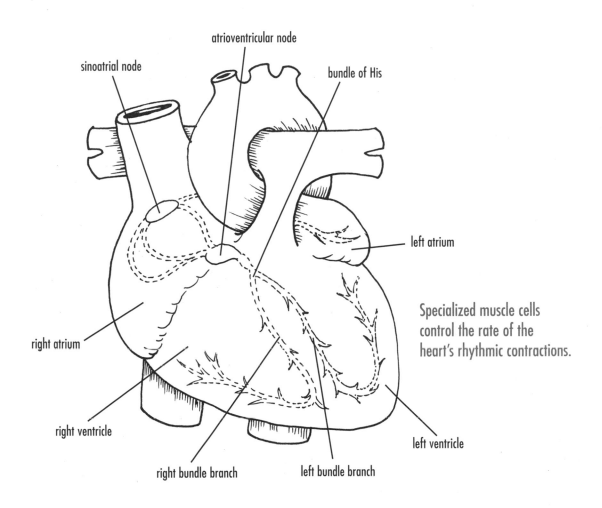

atrioventricular node

sinoatrial node

bundle of His

left atrium

right atrium

Specialized muscle cells control the rate of the heart's rhythmic contractions.

right ventricle

left ventricle

right bundle branch

left bundle branch

Can I learn to control my heart rate?

The action of the heart muscle is ordinarily outside conscious control. But some studies suggest that it is possible to learn to speed or slow the heart. Canadian researchers gave biofeedback training to 46 patients with heart disease. The scientists used a heart monitor to track four electrical patterns that occur simultaneously when the heart beats. One of the patterns reveals a "message" from the nervous system that slows the heart. It dampens the "speed up" signal that increases heart rate when we are depressed, moving fast, or stressed. The volunteers in the study looked at a graph that showed them how much of the relaxing stimulus their hearts were getting. Using deep breathing and relaxation exercises, the people were able to enhance the "slow down" message at will.[64] "Participants learned to control how their heart was being regulated by their nervous system," says University of Toronto scientist Rob Nolan.[65] He thinks that such training might one day be used along with conventional treatments for heart disease.

Lance Armstrong and the Tour de France

. . . . .

In cycling, you see the human engine at the highest expression of ability to endure.[66]

—MAX TESTA,
FORMERLY TEAM DOCTOR TO THE
U.S. TOUR DE FRANCE CYCLING TEAMS

. . . . .

*A*sk a dozen sportscasters who's the greatest quarterback, pitcher, or tennis player of all time, and you'll probably get a dozen different answers. Ask the same question about cycling, and chances are you'll get only one: Lance Armstrong. Armstrong is the champion of the world's toughest bike race, the Tour de France. Two hundred of the world's top cyclists compete in the annual event. On July 23, 2005, 50,000 people stood in the rain to celebrate Armstrong's seventh victory. No other rider had ever managed more than five. "This is a dream come true," Armstrong said.[67]

Few Americans understand how the Tour de France is run. At least six days of the three-week race are spent negotiating the high mountains of the Pyrenees and the Alps. Daily stages of as many as 150 miles (240 km) require the cyclists to travel back roads, highways, cobblestones, and gravel tracks in boiling heat, driving rain, and the occasional hail storm. In the time-trial segments of the race, cyclists go all out against the clock. The race leader at any stage is the rider with the least total time in both the daily stages and the time trials. The competitors are so skilled that a single lapse—for example, falling behind in a single uphill climb—can throw a cyclist out of the race. While the emphasis is on the endurance required to cycle long distances over many days, the race also requires high-intensity effort. During the time trials and mountain climbs, riders are working at 90 percent of their maximal oxygen uptake (VO_{2max}), which is the greatest amount of oxygen an individual can consume in a minute.[68] "I've read that I *flew* up the hills and mountains of France. But you don't fly up a hill. You struggle slowly and painfully up a hill, and maybe, if you work very hard, you get to the top ahead of everybody else," Armstrong says.[69]

Few people question that Armstrong was "born different" from the rest of us. Laboratory tests show that's true. Like other professional cyclists, Armstrong has an especially efficient respiratory system, an enhanced ability to burn fat as an energy source, and a greater than average resistance to fatigue of the slow-twitch motor units.[70] His heart is large and can beat more than 200 times per minute. (Even the fittest, young, male athletes top out at 195.) Armstrong's heart pumps large quantities of blood and oxygen to his leg muscles. His VO_{2max} puts him in the top 1 percent of the population. During strenuous exercise, he builds up in his blood far less lactate, a toxic waste product of muscle action, than the rest of us do.[71] "I can endure more physical stress than most people can, and I don't get as tired while I'm doing it," Armstrong explains.[72]

Armstrong pedals extremely fast, using lower gears than most other cyclists do. He climbs mountains at revolutions often exceeding 110–120 times per minute, compared to the 70–90 most other riders manage. He pushes not in a higher gear, which takes more leg muscle, but at a greater pace, which takes more lung capacity. Over his years of training, he's improved his pedaling actions, wasting less power at the top and the bottom of the turn. He has also learned to remain seated rather than standing on the pedals while climbing mountains.

"Armstrong started with a strong genetic makeup," says Edward Coyle, a scientist who studied Armstrong in the University of Texas-Austin Human Performance Laboratory for eight years. "But he maximized his abilities and got where he is through dedication and hard training."[73] Over that time, Armstrong improved his muscular efficiency by 8 percent. That improvement, along with a 7 percent reduction in fat and body weight, resulted in what Coyle calculated as a whopping 18 percent improvement in his power output.[74] Since only a 1–3 percent difference separates the winner from the middle finisher in most Olympic finals, an 8 percent improvement in efficiency is remarkable.

Despite the studies, how Armstrong was able to improve his efficiency so greatly is not well understood. Coyle thinks Armstrong may have improved the efficiency of ATP turnover in his muscle fibers during contraction. Armstrong may also have increased his percentage of Type I muscle fibers from 60 to 80 percent.[75] Studying other cyclists, Coyle and his colleagues have shown that people who have a high percentage of Type I

Tour de France

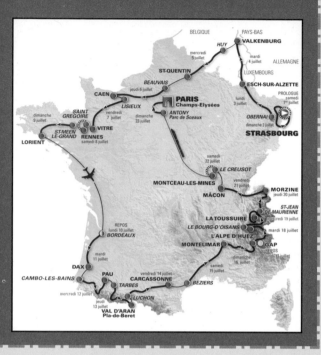

The Tour de France covers more than 2,000 miles (3,200 km) of French countryside in three weeks.

muscle fibers achieve high muscular efficiency when cycling. They generate a greater muscular output per liter of oxygen consumed and per calorie of food energy burned. Coyle has also found that the best cyclists produce greater power on the downstroke of the pedaling motion. This is probably because they have a greater percentage of Type I muscle fibers accompanied by a greater density of blood vessels in their muscles.[76]

Armstrong knows the value of studying muscles. "Cyclists are com-puter slaves," he says. "We hover over precise calculations of cadence, efficiency, force, and wattage. I was constantly sitting on a stationary bike with electrodes all over my body, looking for different positions on the bike that might gain mere seconds, or a piece of equipment that might be a little bit more aerodynamic."[77] But as he claimed his seventh Tour de France victory, Armstrong wasn't thinking about laboratories. "This is a hard sporting event, and hard work wins it," he said.[78]

CHAPTER THREE

ABOUT MUSCLES AND EXERCISE

*Lack of activity destroys the good condition of
every human being, while movement and methodical
physical exercise save it and preserve it.*[79]

—PLATO (C. 427–347 B.C.)

**What makes
muscles strong?**

In general, the bigger a muscle, the stronger
it is. In adolescence, growth hormones cause
muscle cells to increase in size and strength.
Later, when full growth is achieved, an adult
must damage a muscle in order to make it
grow. Strange as it may seem, a muscle's
mass and power increase through the same
process that repairs muscle injuries.

Here's how it works: Exercise causes tiny tears in muscle tissue. In
response, the muscle cell increases the amount of protein it contains.
The damage also attracts satellite cells. These divide and fuse with
existing muscle fibers. That process does not increase the total number
of cells in a muscle, but it does increase the size of the fibers and the
number of nuclei they contain. Because the DNA in the nucleus directs

the manufacture of cell proteins, more nuclei mean more muscle proteins are made. Increased amounts of protein mean more sarcomeres and more crossbridges that generate more force. Thus, greater amounts of protein both enlarge the muscle and increase its strength.

Exercise also increases the number of blood vessels in muscle. Scientists at George Washington University took samples from the muscles of volunteers who performed hundreds of contractions of their legs. They found evidence of "vascular remodeling"—a rapid change in the tiny vessels that provide the muscle's blood supply. They found more proteins being made in the muscle fibers too, especially after the eccentric contractions that damage muscle most.[80]

Endurance exercises that require a sustained effort affect muscle in another way. They increase the number and the size of mitochondria in the cells. Recall that mitochondria are the cell's "power plants," its source of ATP. More and bigger mitochondria mean a larger and more accessible energy supply. The effect is large. Trained runners have 50 percent more of the volume of their leg muscles in mitochondria than "couch potatoes" do.[81]

Exercise can increase muscle fiber size by up to 25 percent,[82] but not all exercise has this effect. Moderate exercise, such as endurance or aerobic training, increases a muscle's ability to sustain activity over a long period of time, but it does not increase muscle size. Muscle growth results from an effort that pushes a muscle to its limit. Children and teens should not, however, try to lift too much weight in hopes of building muscle. "Strength training is safe for kids; power lifting [of very heavy weights] is not," says Dr. Jordan Metzl in *The Young Athlete*. "The bones of children and teens end in open growth plates made of cartilage, and power lifting is potentially dangerous to growth plates. If a child or teen tries to apply a maximum force across the growth plate, he [or she] can pull off the end of the bone; this is called *avulsion fracture*."[83] Surgery may be required to repair it.

How does exercise damage muscle cells?

"Exercise-induced muscle injury in humans frequently occurs after unaccustomed exercise, particularly if the exercise involves a large amount of eccentric contractions," say researchers P. M. Clarkson and M. J. Hubal.[84] One sign of damage in muscle cells is Z-line "streaming." Streaming is scattered, severe widening of the distance between sarcomeres. The amount of inflammatory chemicals (made by the immune system) increases, both within the injured muscle and in the blood. More muscle proteins show up in the blood also, and the exerciser may report feeling muscular soreness.

All these effects seem to lessen after one exercise session. Less soreness (and presumably less damage) occurs in the next. What explains this "repeated bout effect"? Perhaps the muscle recruits more or different motor units to the task. Or maybe the number of sarcomeres working in series increases. Other possible explanations include a lessened inflammatory response or a reduction in the number of fibers susceptible to stress.[85]

What causes muscle fatigue?

Hold a soup can in your hand and extend your arm out in front of you. Holding the can seems easy at first, but after a while, you will feel an irresistible urge to lower your arm. That is muscle fatigue. (Don't confuse it with the general fatigue that makes you feel drowsy and ready for sleep.)

Some scientists think the source of muscle fatigue lies primarily in the muscles themselves. Declining oxygen levels offer one possible explanation. When volunteers exercise on a treadmill until they feel near exhaustion, their rate of oxygen use reaches an upper limit. It won't go any higher, no matter how hard they try. Perhaps reaching that level signals the body that "enough is enough." Another candidate for the fatigue trigger is lactic acid. Its level builds up in muscles the longer and harder they are used. It's possible that some lactic acid "threshold" makes exercisers feel so spent that they know they have to quit. Yet a third possibility is that changing concentrations of phosphate, potassium, or calcium trigger fatigue.

In this "mainly muscles" model of fatigue, the strength of the brain's signal to the muscle increases, but fatigued motor units grow less responsive to it. Nerve impulses recruit more motor units to the task to make up for those that "drop out." Meanwhile, the fatigued units start to recover. If the effort is not too great, a balance is achieved and muscle action can continue. But if too many motor units are fatigued, recovery is not quick enough. "After a period of time, when all motor units in the muscle have developed fatigue and cannot be activated anymore, these muscles are then totally fatigued and the task of producing force or movement cannot be continued," explain researchers J. Z. Liu, R. W. Brown, and G. H. Yue.[86]

Some scientists aren't convinced that muscles are the main cause of fatigue. They think the brain may play a greater role. It may send the "stop now" signal long before the muscles reach their physical limits.[87] To test that theory, South African researchers put well-trained cyclists on exercise bikes. They taped electrodes to the cyclists' legs to measure electrical activity in the muscles. Their hypothesis was this: If individual muscle fibers were hitting some physical limit—such as maximal oxygen use or lactic acid overload—then the number of fibers recruited to the pedaling task should increase as the cyclists worked against muscle fatigue. Their hypothesis proved wrong. The greater the cyclists' fatigue, the less the electrical activity in their legs—even when less than 20 percent of the available muscle tissue was in use.[88]

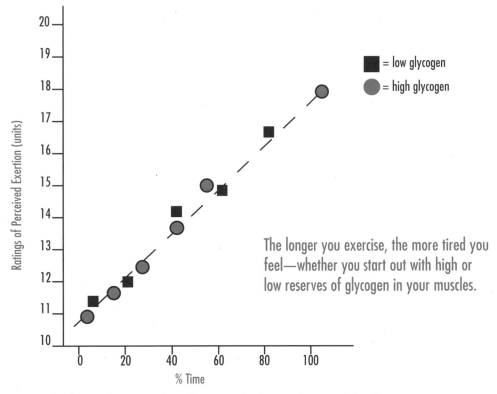

= low glycogen

= high glycogen

The longer you exercise, the more tired you feel—whether you start out with high or low reserves of glycogen in your muscles.

Redrawn from T.D. Noakes, R.J. Snow, and M.A. Febbraio, "Linear Relationship Between the Perception of Effort and the Duration of Constant Load Exercise That Remains," *Journal of Applied Physiology* (April 2004), p. 1572.

"The cyclists may have felt completely done in," researcher Timothy Noakes says, "but their bodies actually had considerable reserves that they could theoretically tap by using a greater fraction of the resting fibers."[89] This, he believes, suggests that the brain stops the muscles long before they become exhausted. "We're finding that a lot of areas of the brain are involved," scientist Alan St Clair Gibson says, "but we haven't yet found the stop switch."[90]

The brain theory may explain why interval training is so effective for runners, cyclists, and other athletes.[91] (Interval training alternates periods of all-out effort with periods of lesser effort, or recovery.) The training doesn't change the structure or chemical activity of muscle. Instead, it may train the brain to accept that working harder is not all that risky.

Is stretching good for muscles?

Stretching is any action that increases the length of a muscle. Stretching before, during, and after exercise may reduce the risk of injury, but more research is needed before we can be sure.[92] What is more certain is that stretching maintains circulation around joints, where injuries are most likely. It increases the muscle's ability to repair the damage that exercise causes—that is, grow bigger and stronger. Stretching reduces the burn that comes from a buildup of lactic acid in the muscle. Stretching also helps you regain normal functioning after an injury. Physical therapists recommend stretches along with strength-building exercises for many of their patients.

Stretching is particularly important for teenagers. The reason is that bones grow faster than muscles. "Kids lose flexibility as they grow because the muscles are constantly trying to keep up with the growing bones," writes sports doctor Jordan Metzl. [93] Losing flexibility makes muscle strains and tendinitis (an overuse injury of the muscle-tendon unit) more likely. Metzl recommends that teens stretch

Stretching improves the flexibility of joints.

their muscles at least three times a week after a good warm-up.

Stretching helps maintain flexibility in the joints and limbs, but it shouldn't be done alone. "Flexibility training should be balanced with strength training to prevent connective tissues from becoming too loose and weak. The key is to strengthen what we stretch and stretch what we strengthen," advises the American College of Sports Medicine.[94] "The bodies of most kids and teens use only 50 to 60 percent of the capacity of the muscles involved in a given activity," Metzl writes. "When a muscle is strength-trained, more of it is utilized."[95]

How important are warm-ups and cool downs?

Here's some good advice from the American College of Sports Medicine:

"Adequate warm-up prior to physical activity is important to ensure a safe and effective exercise session. A simple warm-up will increase blood flow throughout the body, especially to muscles, and will begin to raise the internal body temperature. Warm muscles and tendons are less prone to injury and may improve physical performance. A proper warm-up also helps with mental preparation for exercise. . . .

"The cool-down period following a workout is just as important as the warm-up. This time is used to reduce your heart rate and breathing rate, and to help with recovery following exercise. Performing a cool-down has been shown to decrease light-headedness and prevent pooling of the blood within the muscles, which can lead to fainting and soreness. A cool down also allows waste products to be removed from your muscles, possibly minimizing soreness after activity."[96]

Does muscle strength affect bones?

Exercising when you are young helps protect bone strength when you grow older. Scientists at the University of Connecticut at Storrs studied more than 100 women ages 20–88. They compared those who had been active in sports and recreation since their teen years with their more sedentary peers. They found that the key factor in bone health was muscle mass. "Muscles strengthened by physical activity put more pressure on bones and stimulate their growth," says Jasminka Ilich-Ernst of the university's Bone and Mineral Metabolism Lab. "This is particularly important in childhood, adolescence, and young adulthood," she adds.[97]

How does weightlifting build muscle?

Strength conditioning, such as weightlifting or working out on exercise machines, increases muscle mass. An increase in the mass of a muscle is called hypertrophy. It "is largely the result of increased contractile proteins," says William Evans of the University of Arkansas.[98] "Lifting weights requires that a muscle shorten as it produces force (concentric contraction). Lowering the weight, on the other hand, forces the muscle to lengthen as it produces force [eccentric contraction]."[99] These lengthening muscle contractions produce what Evans calls "ultrastructural damage": microscopic tears in the contractile proteins of muscle cells. Those tears may stimulate the cell to make muscle proteins faster. Although the synthesis of new proteins begins within days, incorporating them into the sarcomeres requires weeks, even months. That's why bodybuilders need patience!

A muscle need not increase in mass to become stronger. When you learn a new movement or place demands on a previously unchallenged muscle, the brain's signal for contraction increases. That recruits more motor units to the task and increases their rate of contraction. Although no increase in muscle size is apparent, strength gains occur because the extent of a muscle's response increases.

What's the best way to build muscle?

It takes resistance to build muscle. Your muscles must work against a weight, as in lifting free weights or working on weight machines. For resistance training to build muscle, the resistance must be significant, such as in lifting a weight that is not easy to lift. On the other hand, attempting to lift too much weight can cause an injury.

To get the maximum benefit with the minimum risk, the American College of Sports Medicine recommends balancing intensity with repetitions. Intensity is the amount of weight lifted. The best range for muscle building is between 65 percent and 75 percent of the maximum possible. For example, if the most you can lift is 50 pounds (about 23 kg), then you can build muscle lifting 30 to 40 pounds (14–18 kg). The number of repetitions you can comfortably perform at this level should be 10–15. So, even without going through a testing program, you can find the right workout level for you. Start with light resistance, and see how many repetitions you can perform, slowly and without stopping. If it is more than 15, try adding a little more resistance. If it's fewer than 10, you are lifting too much.

Darryn Willoughby, exercise expert at Baylor University, recommends one or two (but no more than three) sets of 10–15 repetitions, performed with intervals of several minutes of rest in between. He says training periods of about 30 minutes are best. Take at least one day off between sessions. Take two or three off if you are lifting very heavy weights. Your body needs time and rest to repair and recover.

Does exercise affect the immune system?

Yes, through many complicated pathways that we only partially understand. For example, during exercise, muscle fibers produce a substance called interleukin-6 (IL-6). IL-6 is a myokine. Myokines are substances made and released by contracting skeletal muscles that affect some other organ(s) of the body. Released into the bloodstream, IL-6 stimulates the immune cells of the blood to make chemicals that prevent or

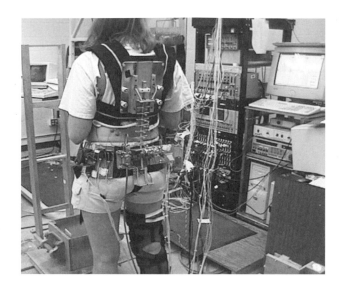

At the Biodynamics Laboratory at Ohio State University, scientists use electronic sensors to study muscle action during exercise.

reduce inflammation. Chronic inflammation is one characteristic of serious diseases, such as heart disease and Type 2 diabetes. Perhaps the action of myokines in blocking that inflammation is the reason why exercise is such good medicine.[100]

Should I take nutritional supplements to build muscle?

No. "Most of us in adolescent medicine think it's best to stay away from these products altogether," says Alison Field, an epidemiologist at Children's Hospital in Boston.[101] Although "protein powders are probably relatively safe," she adds," some of the other products may not be so benign."[102] The Food and Drug Administration does not regulate supplements sold in supermarkets, drugstores, and health food stores. Many supplements fail to deliver on their claims. Some are dangerous or even fatal.

Despite these warnings, many young people turn to supplements in hopes of achieving what they believe to be "the perfect body." Field and her team surveyed more than 10,000 young adults, ages 12 to 18.[103] About 30 percent, both male and female, said they think often about wanting more toned or defined muscles. Field found that those who are most concerned about their body's size, strength, or appearance were the most influenced by magazines and television to try risky or unproven supplements or herbal products. The most often used products were protein powders and shakes. Others, used predominantly by boys, included creatine, amino acids, the amino-acid metabolite HMB, the hormone dehydroepiandrosterone (DHEA), growth hormone, and anabolic steroids.

At best, these supplements are ineffective and a waste of money. At worst, they are dangerous. For example, advertisers often tout creatine as a way to improve performance in high intensity, short duration activities such as sprinting. Their claims may be valid, but we don't know whether taking creatine is safe. No laws guarantee the purity of over-the-counter creatine supplements. In addition, some evidence suggests that creatine causes weight gain, muscle cramps, abdominal cramps, nausea, and diarrhea. It's possible that creatine can cause high blood pressure and loss of kidney function. Creatine supplementation may also increase pressure on muscles, blood vessels, and nerves in the lower leg of an exercising athlete.[104] The pressure can block blood flow and lead to permanent injury.

Field says, "The Internet is full of sites where [supplements] can be purchased, and many are advertised in popular health and fitness magazines."[105] The smartest decision? Ignore them.

Does exercise make the heart muscle larger?

Endurance training (aerobic exercise) increases the mass of the heart. It also increases the volume of the left ventricle, the chamber in the heart that pumps blood to all body parts except the lungs.[106] This improvement in the heart's action has positive health benefits. Most adults have an average resting heart rate of around 60–80 beats per minute. The heart rate of people who get regular exercise can get down to as few as 40 beats per minute. That saves the heart about 50,000 beats a day. As an article in the *Washington Post* explains, "a well-conditioned heart conserves energy and can supply oxygen-rich blood to the rest of the body with half the effort."[107]

This beneficial growth of the heart muscle is not the same as "enlarged heart" disease, in which the volume of the heart increases disproportionately to the amount of blood it can pump.[108] An abnormally enlarged heart is weaker, not stronger. Heart valve disease or high blood pressure can cause the heart to enlarge in this way. So can damage that weakens the muscle, such as a heart attack or the disease called congestive heart failure. An enlarged heart is also a symptom of cardiomyopathy. That's a name for a number of diseases in which the heart muscle fails to function properly.

Why do I get sore when I exercise?

Ed Nessel, the 1998 United States Masters Swimming Coach of the Year, is no stranger to muscle soreness. Anyone who swims competitively "is usually so beat-up that even their eyebrows hurt!" he says. [109] Swimmers aren't the only ones who get sore. "If you overdo any kind of physical effort . . . working out longer than usual or harder than usual . . . about 12 to 48 hours later, you will develop very stiff, sore muscles."[110] This is DOMS, or delayed onset muscular soreness. DOMS may increase in intensity for up to three days. It's usually gone in five to seven.

Sometimes DOMS results from fluid build-up in tissues, muscle spasms, or stretching a muscle or tendon too far. More often, it results from the same microscopic tears in muscles that make them grow bigger and stronger. Devices that detect electrical activity in the muscles show that continuing contraction does not cause the soreness. Instead, it may be a product of shortening—not of the muscle itself, but of tendons and other connective tissues.[111]

Eccentric contractions that lengthen a muscle while it's working against gravity contribute more to DOMS than concentric or isometric contractions. For example, concentric arm flexion exercises (bicep curls) produce less DOMS than arm flexion eccentric exercises (arm extension), but the two together produce the greatest soreness.[112] Along with DOMS comes a temporary loss of strength. "You won't be able to move as well as normal, and you may have swelling," Nessel says.[113] Fast movements are most likely to cause DOMS. "Muscles become sore after faster movement, even if the force and work levels were higher at slower speeds," Nessel explains.[114]

DOMS diminishes with time, and its symptoms can be reduced, if not eliminated. Over-the-counter rubs help some people feel less tenderness. Cold packs reduce swelling. Hot packs after swelling has subsided can accelerate muscle relaxation and increase blood flow, speeding muscle repair.

Warming up before exercise helps prevent DOMS. So does increasing the intensity of exercise gradually. Trainers recommend that people perform several rounds of lower intensity (lighter resistance) eccentric exercise one to six weeks before attempting higher intensity (heavier resistance) eccentric exercises.[115] It's also important to allow adequate time between workouts to promote muscle repair. In the end, the best treatment for DOMS is more of what caused it: exercise. Moving muscles reduces soreness, and building muscle strength lessens the severity of DOMS in the future.[116]

Should I exercise when I hurt?

It depends. There are times when pain tells you to rest, especially after an injury. But too much rest can increase pain and cause loss of fitness, which leads to still more pain and increases the risk of further injury. Moderate exercise can relieve pain, building muscles that support and protect the joints. Moving the joints and stretching the muscles increases flexibility. That reduces stiffness in joints and minimizes pain. With exercise, you sleep better, so tiredness doesn't make your pain worse.

The world-famous Mayo Clinic advises exercising with caution if your muscles are sore and aching—but only if your doctor has given you permission to exercise. You should stop exercising and see your doctor if

- you have swelling around a joint, especially if it's red and warm;
- your joint pain worsens with exercise;
- you have a fever without a specific illness;
- you have pain when you bear weight, especially pain that causes you to limp;
- the joint feels unstable, or there's a block to joint motion, such as a "locked" knee;
- your pain doesn't improve or it gets worse. [117]

The Straight Scoop on Steroids

. . . . .

The strongest thing I put into my body is steak and eggs....
Steroids are not even a thought.[118]
—JIM THOME, PROFESSIONAL BASEBALL PLAYER

. . . . .

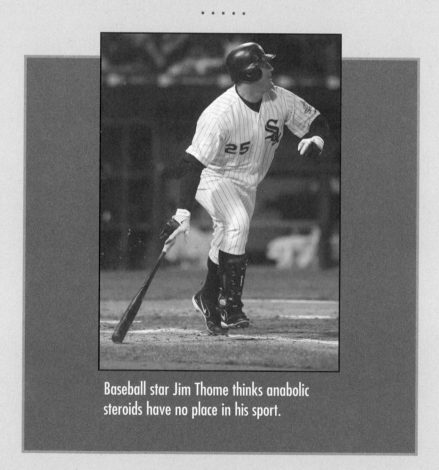

Baseball star Jim Thome thinks anabolic
steroids have no place in his sport.

Open up the sports section of your favorite newspaper or switch on your favorite sports channel. Chances are you'll read or hear about a steroid scandal. *What are steroids, anyway?* you may wonder. *What's all the fuss about?*

To answer those questions, let's first clear up the confusion about the definition of a steroid. The term actually includes several different types of compounds. The body makes some of them naturally. The adrenal cortex of the brain releases three steroids: cortisol (a stress hormone), aldosterone (a sodium-retaining hormone that regulates blood pressure), and testosterone (the main sex hormone in males—although females make some too). Of those three, only testosterone affects muscles. It is a natural anabolic (muscle-building) steroid.

The anabolic steroids that some athletes take (usually illegally and against the rules of their sport) are derivatives of testosterone. Their molecules bind to receptor sites in the cytoplasm of cells and form a complex that migrates into the nucleus. There the steroid acts on DNA, the master molecule of the cell. It alters what genes are expressed, as well as when

and how. In muscle cells, the natural action of testosterone is to promote muscle building. Anabolic steroids have the same effect if taken as a drug.

In bones, anabolic steroids taken as drugs change into estrogen. Estrogen is the main female hormone (but males have some too). Estrogen causes growth plates in the bones to close. Normally that closure occurs in the teens or early twenties after growth is finished. Taking steroid drugs to build muscle before age 20 causes growth plates to close early. The steroid user ends up shorter than he or she would have been. In males, taking anabolic steroids causes the testicles to shrink and sperm production to decline. Because the steroid is changed to estrogen, breasts grow in males—a condition called gynecomastia.[119] Other side effects include mood swings, hallucinations, paranoia, liver and kidney damage, high blood pressure, and an increased risk for heart disease, stroke, and some forms of cancer. Withdrawal often brings on depression.

Steroids increase aggressive feelings and actions. The increased aggression is sometimes called "'roid rage." Scientist Richard Melloni Jr. of Northeastern University in Boston studied adolescent hamsters. The animals' aggressive behavior increased when they were taking steroids. It continued for weeks after they stopped. Melloni found permanent changes in the animals' brains as a result of steroid use.[120] He thinks the same changes occur in humans. "Steroids step on the gas for aggression," Melloni says. "Muscle mass and medals aren't worth the risk of hurting someone or landing in jail."[121]

Although most of what we hear and read about anabolic steroids is negative, doctors do sometimes prescribe the drugs. "Anabolic steroids have a very limited scope of legal use here in the United States," says Kevin Plancher, orthopaedic surgeon of the U.S. ski and snowboard teams.[122] For example, some patients suffering from illnesses such as AIDS can develop chronic wasting disease. They lose weight and muscle mass and can't regain either no matter how much they eat or exercise. Evidence suggests that anabolic steroids can help them increase both lean body mass and total body weight.[123] Researchers are also exploring the use of anabolic steroids to treat lung diseases and infertility.

To treat a variety of illnesses, doctors prescribe some other kinds of steroid drugs that have nothing to do with building muscle. The best known are the corticosteroids. Chemically, they are very different from anabolic steroids. "Corticosteroids are vital to the practice of medicine," Plancher says.[124] "Because they exhibit potent anti-inflammatory effects, they are used most commonly to treat arthritis, as well as short-term inflammation associated with orthopaedic injuries," he says.[125] "Corticosteroids are also widely used to treat asthma, in both inhalant and oral applications."[126] In addition, they are popular active ingredients in creams used to treat rashes and other skin disorders.

Plancher points out that doctors use steroids effectively and legally to treat many medical conditions. The key is in differentiating these drugs from anabolic steroid drugs that are apt to do more harm than good. "We want to avoid the common misperception that all steroids are alike," he says. "But at the same time, we also must stress that any time a patient is taking any kind of steroid, he or she should be closely monitored by a physician."[127]

ADVERSE EFFECTS OF ANABOLIC STEROIDS[128]

Males	Females	Both Males and Females
baldness	breast shrinkage	acne
prostate changes	enlargement of the clitoris	aggression
breast enlargement	increased facial and body hair	brittle connective tissue
impotence (inability to achieve an erection)	irregularities in the menstrual period	heart disease
sterility (inability to produce sperm)	hair loss	stroke
	thickening of the vocal cords, leading to a low-pitched voice	physical or psychological dependency (addiction)
		headaches
		high blood pressure
		liver disease
		changes in thoughts and behavior
		short stature (because growth plates close too soon)

CHAPTER FOUR

QUESTIONS

ABOUT INJURIES AND DISEASES

Everyone who is born holds dual citizenship, in the kingdom of the well and in the kingdom of the sick. Although we all prefer to use only the good passport, sooner or later each of us is obliged, at least for a spell, to identify ourselves as citizens of that other place.[129]

—SUSAN SONTAG, *ILLNESS AS METAPHOR*, 1977

How do muscles get injured?

Muscle injuries fall into two broad categories: acute and overuse. Acute injuries result from a single trauma, such as pivoting too fast when playing basketball or falling in gymnastics training.

Overuse injuries are just what their name suggests: a muscle becomes painful from being used too much. In all sports, overuse injuries account for perhaps 30 to 50 percent of all injuries.[130] They occur most often in those who are new to an activity and who attempt too much, too soon. Performing a movement in the wrong way invites an overuse injury. That's why coaches and trainers are fussy about form.

The most common injuries associated with running are overuse injuries. "Knees are the most common body part injured, followed by feet, ankles, lower legs and shins, upper legs, back and hips," says James Herndon, past-president of the American Academy of Orthopaedic Surgeons.[131] Doctors often see patients who have

- *a hamstring tear,* or a break in the muscle at the back of the thigh that flexes the knee. Hamstring injuries plague joggers who suddenly sprint. The agonist-antagonist relationship between muscles in the leg is altered too quickly, and the hamstring—being the weaker of the pair—tears as a result.

- *shin splints,* a general term for muscle problems in the lower leg, which, if not treated, can progress to a stress fracture. Shin splints plague flat-footed runners. The muscles of the lower leg work overtime if the muscles that hold up the arch of the foot aren't working properly.

- *plantar fasciitis,* inflammation of the tendons in the foot. Tendons can rip away from their attachment to the heel bone, compressing nerves and causing extreme pain.[132]

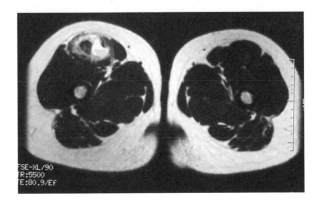

These MRI (magnetic resonance imaging) pictures show the rectus femoris muscle of the thigh. The one on the right is normal. The white area near the top in the left picture reveals a tear in the muscle.

Treatment for an overuse injury usually means resting the painful muscle totally or at least partially for a while. However, prevention is better than any treatment. Proper warm-ups and cool downs help prevent overuse injuries, as does maintaining a healthy weight and a good level of overall fitness.

What are sprains and strains?

A sprain is not a muscle injury but an injury to a ligament, the rope of connective tissue that holds a joint together. One example is twisting an ankle while playing basketball. A sharp pivot can overstretch a ligament and cause pain and impaired movement. Some sprains are mild and heal quickly. Others can be severe and require medical attention.

Strains are muscle injuries. An example is pulling a hamstring in a baseball game. Strains also vary from mild to severe. In mild cases, the basic structure of the muscle is unchanged. In more serious cases, the muscle tears. It may also be bruised or inflamed.

What's the best first aid for muscle injuries?

Remember the mnemonic: **R. I. C. E.** [133]

R = Rest: Resting an injured area is necessary to allow the body time to get the effects of the trauma under control. It also helps to avoid additional stress and damage to the injured tissue. The period of rest required will vary depending on the severity of the injury. People who do not rest an acute injury can prolong the inflammation period and increase the healing time required, thereby delaying the recovery.

I = Ice: Ice applied promptly to an injury can slow down or minimize some of the inflammation. The cold causes a closing of the arterioles (small blood vessels) in the tissue, which reduces any internal bleeding that may be occurring. The local tissue metabolism slows down, reducing the tissue's need for oxygen and nutrients, and the nerve impulses are slowed to reduce the pain that's felt, providing a numbing effect.

C = Compression: Compression is the application of a bandage or wrap around the injured area. The bandage's purpose is to help control swelling and to provide mild support. Apply the bandage carefully. Too tight a bandage could disrupt the circulation of blood to the area.

E = Elevation: This involves raising the injured area above the level of the heart whenever possible. This position lets gravity and the lymphatic system work together to drain away fluids and reduce swelling.

What causes muscle cramps?

A cramp is an involuntary muscle contraction that lasts and hurts. It is sometimes called a spasm. Cramps result from different causes. Overexertion is often the trigger. Loss of fluids or potassium in the blood—which can occur, for example, during a long or strenuous race—can bring on a cramp.

Drinking water can sometimes relieve cramps. So can gentle stretching and massage. Eating bananas and oranges can replenish lost potassium, but salt tablets—which some people take seeking relief from muscle cramps—can actually make things worse. Salt draws water from the blood stream into the stomach, causing dehydration and further cramping. Some cramps have nothing to do with exercise. Pregnant women, for instance, sometimes experience cramps in their legs because of shifting calcium levels in their blood.

What causes a stitch?

A stitch is a sudden, sharp pain felt in the side or abdomen during exercise. It happens because the body diverts blood to the skeletal muscles, starving the abdominal muscles of oxygen. Stitches most often affect those unaccustomed to exercise when they run more than they are used to.

What is a hernia?

A hernia is a condition in which part of the intestine pokes through a hole in the muscles of the abdominal wall. Women sometimes get hernias, but they are more common in men. When a male fetus is developing in its mother's womb, its testicles form inside the lower abdomen. Sometime before birth, the testicles move downward into the scrotum. A small muscle called the cremaster descends with them. (Males can feel this muscle in action. In cold places or scary situations, the cremaster reflexively raises the testicles into the scrotum, providing warmth and protecting against injury.[134]) The descending of the testicles leaves a small hole in the lower abdomen. Normally, the hole closes and seals. But if it remains open, a part of the intestine can poke through. If the intestine is pinched tight, it can lose its blood supply. The area can become infected.

What causes back pain?

Pain in the back, especially the low back, is common. About 80 percent of us experience it at one time or another. It's the second most frequent reason for visiting a doctor, the fifth most frequent cause of hospitalization, and the third most frequent reason for surgery. Half of those who experience an episode of low back pain have another episode within a year. For many people, low back pain is an on-again-off-again problem throughout life. [135]

Back pain has many sources. It can come from strained ligaments, damaged joints, damage to the discs that cushion the bones of the spine, or overstretched or overtight back muscles. If a nerve from the spinal cord gets pinched or inflamed, the muscles tense, causing low back pain. Heavy lifting, poor posture, and sitting too much are common causes. According to Jessica Smith of *American Fitness* magazine, "up to 80 to 90 percent of low back pain has been attributed to improper posture, poor body mechanics, and weak or imbalanced musculature."[136]

The most severe back pain typically results from herniating, or rupturing, a disc in the spine. Discs are not muscles but soft structures that lie between the vertebrae of the back. They are something like a plastic bag full of Jell-O. They prevent the bones from rubbing together; they cushion the impact of movement. They also make bending the spine possible. Their wedge shape gives the normal spine its S-curve shape. A sudden injury or prolonged pressure on a disc can compress it enough that the outer casing breaks. When it does, some of the gelatinous fluid leaks out. The fluid can then press on a nerve, causing pain. If the fluid presses on the sciatic nerve, it produces shooting pains in the legs called sciatica.

Whatever its cause, back pain breeds more back pain. In an unconscious effort to avoid it, back pain sufferers change the way they use their back muscles. Scientist William Marras and his team at Ohio State University measured stresses on the spine during lifting. They compared the stresses in people who had back pain and those who did not. They found that compression of the spine and twisting force were greater for those with pain.[137] "People with back pain guard the injured area by using more muscles than they need to, but those extra muscles are not necessarily all working together," Marras told the *New York Times*. "It's as if they're pushing down on the short end of the seesaw and trying to lift something on the far end."[138]

The first aid for back pain is the same as for any other muscle injury. "Lie down on your back and relax 20 to 30 minutes," says orthopaedic specialist William Lauerman of Georgetown University Hospital. "Ice packs should help reduce initial pain and swelling. If your back pain continues, you may require medical attention."[139] Anti-inflammatory medications such as acetaminophen or ibuprofen can relieve discomfort. Walking and losing weight can reduce the risks of future episodes. So can exercises that strengthen the abdominal muscles, because they support the low back.

Doctors sometimes prescribe painkilling drugs or injections as short-term solutions for back pain. Long-term, it's best to stay active and strengthen back muscles. Exercise can't cure back pain,[140] but it does help maintain strength, endurance, and bone density—all of which can be lost from too much resting of muscles.[141] Physical therapy may help patients with severe or long-lasting back pain return to their normal daily activities.

Do *muscles cause tension headaches?*

The International Headache Society defines a tension-type headache (T-TH) as the opposite of a migraine. The sufferer feels pain on both sides of the head. The pain is steady, not pulsating. It's not severe enough to bring a halt to daily activity. The only symptom is head pain. No visual disturbances or stomach upsets go along with a T-TH.

T-TH is associated with tenderness of the muscles of the head and neck, although there may not be any measurable contractile activity of those muscles. The more tenderness, the worse the headache. Although the sufferer feels pain in the forehead, around the eyes, at the temples, and (to a lesser degree) in the cheeks, the muscle stiffness lies elsewhere. The pain, then, is "referred." That means it originates in one place but is felt in another. One study found in T-TH sufferers a 40 percent increase in the stiffness of the trapezius muscle and a 15 percent increase in stiffness of other muscles at the back of the neck. Other sources of the referred pain include several muscles in the jaw and the sternocleidomastoid that runs from behind the ear down to the collarbone and breastbone.[142]

Most of us treat our T-THs with over-the-counter pain relievers. Doctors can offer prescription medicines and alternative treatments in frequent and severe cases. The long-term solution for most of us is to relieve the psychological distress that invokes the muscle tenderness in the first place.

What recreational activities result in the most injuries?

Be careful the next time you ride a bike. Among children and young teens, bike riding rates number one on the list of injuries of all types, as well as injuries of the bones and muscles. Basketball, football, and roller sports (including in-line skating, skateboarding, and roller-skating) rank two, three, and four, followed by playground accidents, baseball/softball, soccer, and jumping on trampolines. The graph on the following page shows the rest.[143] As you study it, keep in mind that these numbers do not take into account the numbers of people participating in these activities. So, one reason for the frequency of cycling injuries is that so many people ride bikes.

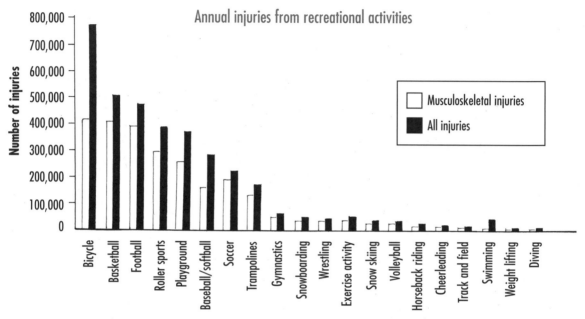

Annual injuries from recreational activities

Legend: Musculoskeletal injuries / All injuries

Reprinted with permission from: John M. Purvis, MD, and Ronald G. Burke, MD, "Recreational Injuries in Children: Incidence and Prevention" (*J Am Acad Orthop Surg*, Vol 9, No 6, November/December 2001, 365–374.)

What school sports produce the most injuries?

Any student who plays a sport faces a risk of injury, but some sports are riskier than others.[144] The National Athletic Trainers' Association reports that the highest injury rate in high school sports occurs among football players. Nearly 35 percent sustain some kind of injury in a season. Boys' wrestling is a close second (27 percent), and girls' soccer is third (26 percent).

The Association classifies the injuries as

General trauma: scrapes, bruises, cuts, painful joints, cramps, spasms, and others;

Sprains: injuries to ligaments, usually resulting from trauma such as falling or twisting;

Strains: injuries to muscles and tendons, usually resulting from overuse, repetitive motions, prolonged positions, or excessive muscle contraction;

Fractures: broken or damaged bones;

Others: nerve injuries, blisters, sunburns, and more.

The circle graphs show the frequency of the injury categories in two sports: boys' baseball, in which muscle strains account for nearly a third of all injuries, and girls' basketball, where muscle strains are less likely in comparison to the far greater risk of sprains. The bar graph on the following page shows the risk of muscle strain for individual girls' and boys' sports. Boys who play football are most likely to strain a muscle. The lowest risk goes to female field hockey players.

Muscle strains account for nearly a third of the injuries in boys' baseball. Muscle strains are less likely than sprains among girls who play baseball.

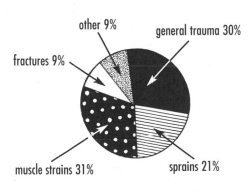

Types of Injuries (%): Boys' Baseball

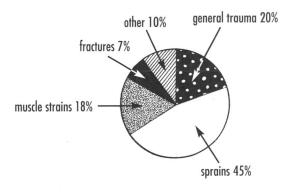

Types of Injuries (%): Girls' Baseball

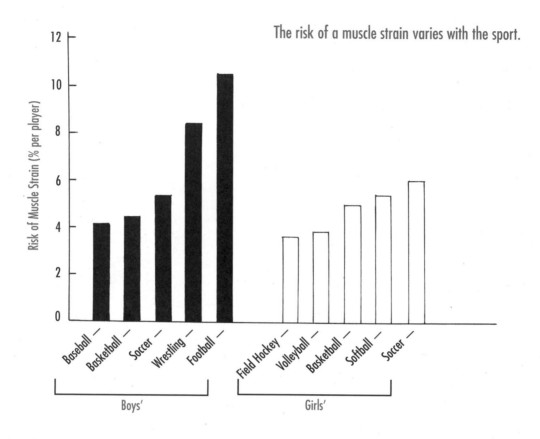

The risk of a muscle strain varies with the sport.

Risk of Muscle Strain (% per player)

Baseball — Basketball — Soccer — Wrestling — Football —

Field Hockey — Volleyball — Basketball — Softball — Soccer —

Boys'

Girls'

Can I overtrain for sports?

Exercising and participating in sports are so good for most of us that we sometimes forget it's possible to overdo. But some people do train too hard. Ten to 20 percent of athletes experience the syndrome called overtraining.[145] When this happens, performance declines. The athlete finds it harder and harder to carry out exercise or to recover from it.

The symptoms of overtraining include

- feeling tired and performing poorly
- taking a long time to recover after training or competition
- feeling irritable, depressed, or unmotivated
- soreness and stiffness in muscles and joints
- stomach aches, colds and flu, muscle pains, elevated resting pulse rate
- insomnia
- loss of appetite and weight loss
- overuse injuries.[146]

Overtraining is highly individual. A training regimen that works well for one athlete may induce overtraining in another. The only treatment is rest. Recovery may require weeks or months. Preventing overtraining is easier than treating it. Allow recovery time between training sessions. Eat healthful foods, drink plenty of water, and don't take on too much. If progress seems slow, just remember that it's better to go at your own pace than to overdo things and miss out entirely.

Can I work too hard at building muscle?

Yes. Aside from the obvious risk of injury, it's possible to develop a psychological disorder called muscle dysmorphia.[147] If you are spending countless hours lifting weights in hopes of "beefing up," you may be at risk. People who have this disorder feel weak and puny no matter how strong they get. They may wear baggy clothing to hide what they believe to be a shameful body. They avoid social contact because they believe their bodies are not acceptable to others.

They spend hours every day thinking about their muscles. Many feel that they have no control over their compulsive muscle-building routines.[148] People who have muscle dysmorphia are more likely than others to sustain overuse injuries, adopt extreme dietary habits, and take dangerous drugs such as anabolic steroids.[149]

Although women can have the disorder, it is much more common in men. In fact, many men show subtle signs even if they aren't obsessive bodybuilders. In one study, Massachusetts psychiatrist Harrison Pope asked American and European men to look at pictures and select what they considered the "ideal" male body type. The men picked bodies that carried about 28 pounds (13 kilograms) more muscle than the men themselves had. The men also told Pope that women find heavy muscles attractive. In fact, numerous studies have shown that women prefer male bodies of average size. Heavy muscles are a turn-off.[150]

Muscle dysmorphia can be treated. Those who have it should seek help. Doctors often recommend counseling and prescribe antidepressants.

My mom had surgery for a torn rotator cuff. What's that?

The big bone of the upper arm (the humerus) joins the shoulder bone (the scapula) in a ball-and-socket joint that allows movement in all directions. Unlike a similar joint at the hip, which is held together with strong ligaments, the shoulder joint is supported mostly by four large muscles. These muscles are the rotator cuff. The muscles of the rotator cuff pass over the top, front, and back of the shoulder joint. Along with the biceps of the upper arm and the deltoids (which lie on top of the shoulder and give it its rounded appearance), they produce the major movements of the upper arm.

Age, overuse, or an accident can tear one or more of the rotator cuff muscles. The shoulder can hurt on the top where the deltoid muscle lies, or at the sides, especially when the arm is raised or extended. Pain when lying down to sleep is also common, because the shoulder joint compresses when the direction of gravity's pull changes. The shoulder may feel weak. It may make a clicking sound when moved. Many doctors use a series of MRI (magnetic resonance

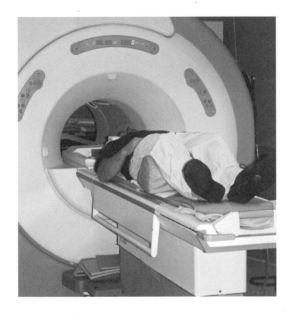

An MRI machine uses a powerful magnet and radio waves to take pictures inside the body. It can help diagnose injuries to muscles and tendons.

imaging) pictures to diagnose a tear in the rotator cuff. They may also use a test called an arthrogram.

Doctors often repair bad tears surgically. Lesser injuries may heal with rest, cold and hot packs, and drugs that relieve inflammation and pain. Sometimes electrical stimulation, ultrasound treatments, or cortisone injections make surgery unnecessary. Physical therapy and exercises—either instead of or after surgery—can improve strength and flexibility.

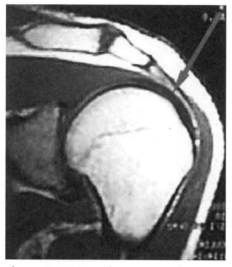 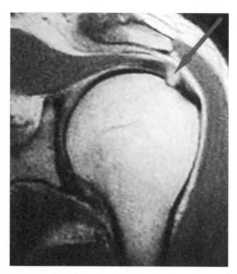

These MRI pictures show a normal rotator cuff (left) and a torn one (right).

How can I prevent muscle injuries?

Use the mnemonic **R. E. S. T. S.**

- **Rest:** Don't train or compete when you feel tired or when your muscles are fatigued or painful.
- **Eat right:** Don't skimp on complex carbohydrates such as fruits, vegetables, and whole-grain breads and cereals. Your muscles need them for energy. Don't skimp on proteins either. Your body uses them to build muscle. Your body gets protein from animal foods such as fish, chicken, and milk. You can also get protein from combinations of plant foods such as beans and rice. When you are active, it's a good idea to eat something nutritious about three hours before you train or compete. And don't forget water. Staying hydrated is essential, especially in endurance sports.

- **Skill:** Get good at your sport. The greater your skill, the less your risk of injury. Know the rules of your sport and follow them. Use protective equipment such as helmets and kneepads.
- **Time:** Go slowly. Don't try to do too much, too soon. Take time for proper warm-ups, cool downs, and stretching.
- **Strength:** Increase your strength. The stronger your muscles, the less prone they are to injury.

What is tendinitis and how is it treated?

Tendinitis is inflammation of a tendon. Overuse is the most common cause—thus "swimmer's shoulder," "jumper's knee," and "tennis elbow." The usual symptoms of tendinitis are pain in the tendon that worsens with activity. First aid for tendinitis is the same as for strains and sprains: rest, ice, compression, and elevation. Doctors may prescribe physical therapy or anti-inflammatory drugs to relieve tendinitis. The best treatment is prevention. Sports doctors recommend strength training before sports seasons begin and good warm-ups and stretching before activity.

A tear in a tendon is more serious than tendinitis. A common sports injury is a tear of the plantaris tendon in the calf. These tears usually heal quickly. Greater problems result from a tear in the Achilles tendon at the back of the heel. The Achilles tendon can bear up to seven times the body's weight without injury, making it the strongest tendon in the body.[151] Nevertheless, it often gets injured, probably because of the force that is placed on it during walking and running.[152] If it is stretched too far while contracting at the same time—as in a sudden movement—it may rupture. Immobilization in a cast or surgery may be needed to repair it.

A myopathy is any disorder of skeletal muscle that is not related to a nerve disorder. Myopathy is not a single disorder but a group of similar disorders. The main thing they have in common is muscle weakness. Other symptoms may include pain, cramps, stiffness, and spasms. Myopathies can be inherited (such as the muscular dystrophies) or acquired. Hormonal dysfunctions, drug abuse, binge drinking, or chemical poisoning can bring on myopathy, as can injury or inflammation. Some kinds of myopathies result from attacks of the immune system on the body's own muscle proteins. Some result from infectious diseases such as influenza and Lyme disease.

Disorders classified as myopathies include

- *congenital myopathies:* Present at birth, these disorders cause muscle weakness, poor muscle tone, and delays in the development of motor skills such as crawling and walking.
- *mitochondrial myopathies:* Abnormalities in mitochondria cause these disorders. They arise from mutations (changes) in mitochondrial DNA.
- *glycogen storage diseases of muscle:* Mutations in genes controlling enzymes that metabolize glycogen and glucose cause these disorders.
- *cardiac myopathies:* Mutations and other conditions cause abnormalities in muscle proteins that lead to weakening of the heart muscle and enlargement of the heart.
- *muscular dystrophies:* These disorders are nearly always inherited and characterized by progressive weakness of the voluntary muscles. (See next question.)

Treatments for myopathies depend on the cause and the symptoms. Some individuals experience few symptoms and little, if any, disability. Medicines, special diets, or exercise programs may relieve symptoms. For other people, however, a myopathy may be disabling or fatal. Treatments for people with severe myopathy include prescription medicines, physical therapy, braces to support weakened muscles, and surgery.

What is muscular dystrophy and how is it treated?

Muscular dystrophy (MD) is not a single disease, but a group of diseases. Most are inherited. None is contagious. All cause skeletal muscles to weaken and degenerate. A few also affect organs other than muscles, including the brain.[153] The most common types are as follows:

- *Duchenne MD* is a sex-linked, genetic disease. (Sex-linked means the gene is inherited on the X chromosome, one of the structures in the nucleus of cells that carries DNA.) It seldom affects girls. The disorder usually appears in boys between three and five years of age. The decline of muscle structure and function is rapid. Most boys with Duchenne MD become unable to walk by age 12. By age 20, they need a respirator to support breathing. This disorder affects about 1 in every 4,000 males.[154]
- *Facioscapulohumeral MD* is present at birth, but its symptoms don't usually appear until adolescence. The disorder causes increasing weakness in muscles of the arms, legs, and face. It progresses slowly. Its symptoms can vary from mild to severe. It is inherited from a parent who has the disorder, although the source cannot be traced in as many as one-third of cases. The disease is thought to affect about 1 in every 20,000 people.[155]

- *Myotonic MD* varies in the age of onset. Its most obvious symptoms are spasms of the muscles in the fingers and face and an irregular gait when walking. Unlike other muscular dystrophies, myotonic MD is accompanied by an inability to relax affected muscles. Abnormalities of the eyes, heart, and endocrine glands also develop. It's inherited as a defect in a muscle enzyme. The cause is an extra repeat of a segment of DNA on either chromosome 19 or chromosome 3. It is the most common form of MD in adults. It affects about 30,000 people in the United States.[156]

Several of the muscular dystrophies, including Duchenne, result from a change in the gene that controls how cells make the protein dystrophin. Dystrophin is a building block of muscle fibers. "Losing dystrophin is like losing the foundation of your house," says Paul Martin, a neuroscientist at the University of California, San Diego. "Without that foundation, the house falls apart."[157] The cause of myotonic dystrophy is a defect in the way that nerve impulses trigger muscle contraction. The signal "stays on" too long so that a contraction, once started, does not stop when it should.[158] Still other forms of MD result from a defect in the way muscles repair damage after exercise.[159]

About 50,000 Americans have some form of muscular dystrophy.[160] There is currently no cure, but the symptoms may be relieved. Respiratory therapy aids breathing. Physical therapy can prevent or reduce muscle pain. Braces can assist leg and arm movement. Surgery can sometimes improve limb function, and a pacemaker can regulate heartbeat. Corticosteroid drugs such as prednisone, which mimic the body's natural hormone cortisone, can slow muscle deterioration.[161] Other drugs can help relax muscles after contraction.

Can gene therapy treat muscular dystrophy?

Gene therapy is any of several methods used to alter or replace genes in cells in order to treat a disorder. Many research teams are working to develop ways of halting or reversing the disease processes of the muscular dystrophies. Researchers often work with mice that have been bred as animal models of human MD. In their experiments, scientists look for ways to change how genes make proteins or to introduce normal genes into cells with missing or mutated genes.

Gene therapies can take any of several forms. One approach might be to let a harmless virus "infect" muscle cells with the normal dystrophin gene. That technique has proved difficult because the gene for dystrophin is one of the largest human genes. Viruses typically used in gene therapy research are too small to carry it. So researchers have created a miniature version of the gene. It has proved effective—in mice at least—in reversing some of the loss of heart muscle that occurs in 90 percent of those who have Duchenne MD.[162]

Another idea is to change the virus that carries the gene. University of Michigan researchers have developed a "stripped-down" carrier virus that has most of its own genetic material removed, making plenty of room for the dystrophin gene.[163] "We have induced long-term expression of the full-sized dystrophin protein for at least three months in the muscles of adult mice with Duchenne muscular dystrophy," reports geneticist Jeffrey Chamberlain.[164]

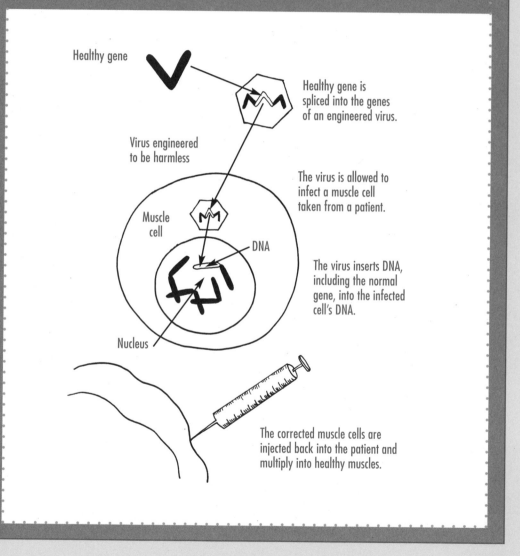

Healthy gene

Healthy gene is spliced into the genes of an engineered virus.

Virus engineered to be harmless

The virus is allowed to infect a muscle cell taken from a patient.

Muscle cell

DNA

Nucleus

The virus inserts DNA, including the normal gene, into the infected cell's DNA.

The corrected muscle cells are injected back into the patient and multiply into healthy muscles.

Two different diseases bear the name myasthenia. One is congenital myasthenia. The other is myasthenia gravis. They are not the same, but they share some symptoms. Both cause muscle weakness and feelings of extreme fatigue. Both result from an abnormality at the junction where nerve meets muscle. However, the specific defect varies between the two diseases and even within subtypes of each disease.

Congenital myasthenia is genetic. Symptoms usually appear at birth or in early childhood. They may include drooping eyelids and weakness of the muscles in the face and limbs. Congenital myasthenia is inherited from one or both parents, although parents often show no signs of the disorder. More than one dozen forms are known.[165] Some involve defects in receptors for acetylcholine on the muscle cell membrane. They can be treated with drugs that enhance the communication between nerve cells and muscle cells.

Myasthenia gravis is an autoimmune disorder. Between 53,000 and 60,000 people in the United States have it.[166] Autoimmune disorders occur when the immune system "makes a mistake." Instead of limiting its attacks to foreign invaders, such as viruses that cause disease, antibodies (immune proteins) attack healthy tissues and organs.

In myasthenia gravis, antibodies attack a muscle protein. In one type, the attack is against the acetylcholine receptors of muscle cells. Certain proteins of the immune system, called antibodies, stick to the receptors. They do more than block the receptors. They mark them for destruction by the immune system. In another type of myasthenia gravis, antibodies attack titin. Titin is a protein in the muscle fiber that helps form the shape of the sarcomere and maintain its function. In yet another form of the disease, antibodies attack kinase. Kinase is an enzyme that is essential to the transfer of energy from ATP.[167]

Symptoms of myasthenia gravis may include muscle weakness, difficulty swallowing, or double vision. The disorder usually develops between the ages of 20 and 50. More women than men are affected, and females tend to develop symptoms at a younger age than males do.[168] Unlike the myopathies, myasthenia gravis does not cause the muscles to degenerate.

Be careful! Don't eat too much licorice. Over-consumption lowers potassium in the blood and causes muscle weakness.

Treatments for myasthenia gravis often include medications that reduce inflammation and suppress the immune system. Drugs can increase the concentration of acetylcholine at the neuromuscular junction, so there is more neurotransmitter available to lock onto the receptor sites that remain healthy.[169] Another treatment is plasmapheresis or plasma exchange. The patient's blood flows through a device that separates blood cells from the liquid portion of the blood, called plasma. The cells are returned to the person, but the plasma—where the antibodies that destroy muscle cells are carried—is replaced.

What is myositis and how is it treated?

Myositis is inflammation of a muscle. Its most obvious symptoms are swelling, tenderness to the touch, and pain. It can have any of several causes, including injury, infection, parasitic infestation, or even strenuous exercise. The swelling of temporary myositis subsides with rest or when the injury or infection is treated.

More serious are the inflammatory myopathies. They have myositis as a symptom, but they also cause a loss of muscle mass. These disorders, which include dermatomyositis and polymyositis, are autoimmune diseases. (See previous question.) They occur when disease-fighting weapons of the immune system—whether T cells, antibodies, or the proteins called complement—attack the tiny blood vessels that supply muscles with food and oxygen. The reduced blood supply damages muscle tissue. It's possible that a viral infection triggers the autoimmune response.[170]

Early signs of chronic myositis may include difficulty in moving, swallowing, or breathing. Joint and muscle pain are common, as are fever and weight loss. A rash is a symptom of dermatomyositis. Both disorders are treated with corticosteroid drugs and plasma exchange.

Are any muscle diseases infectious?

Viruses, bacteria, fungi, or parasitic worms can cause some muscle diseases. The formation of abscesses in the muscles is called pyomyositis. It's a disease of the tropics. It occurs when a bacterial infection spreads through the blood. It's treated with antibiotics. Gas gangrene is an infection of dead muscle that can lead to amputation. It's often attributed to the bacterium *Clostridium botulinum*. Poliomyelitis (polio or infantile paralysis) is *not* technically a muscle disease. It is a viral infection of the spinal cord. The virus destroys the nerves that stimulate the skeletal muscles to contract.

The disease trichinellosis (or trichinosis) develops when the roundworm *Trichinella* invades muscle tissue. This disease begins when humans eat undercooked meat that contains the encysted larvae of the worm. The larvae are released from their cysts when they are exposed to acids and enzymes in the digestive system. Then they burrow into the wall of the small intestine, develop into adult worms, and mate. After about one week, the females release larvae that travel to skeletal muscle, where some species of *Trichinella* form cysts. Symptoms include fever, swelling, and muscle pain, although many people have no symptoms. The disease can be treated with drugs.

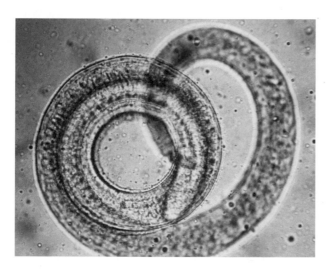

This is a larva of *Trichinella*, freed from its cyst. It is about 1 millimeter long.

Trichinellosis persists because the worm infects wild rodents. Farm and game animals contract the worm when they eat carrion. They can then pass it on to humans who don't cook the meat well enough. Trichinellosis was once associated with eating undercooked pork, but strict food safety laws have reduced the risk of commercial pork. Most cases now result from eating undercooked game meats, such as bear, cougar, or wild boar.[171]

Are cerebral palsy and multiple sclerosis muscle diseases?

No. Although both involve problems of movement, posture, and coordination, the muscles are normal. The cause of both diseases lies in the brain or nervous system. Cerebral palsy is caused by damage to the motor-control area of the brain. The damage usually occurs before birth or in premature infants, often because of a lack of oxygen to the brain or bleeding in the brain. Multiple sclerosis is a disease of the nervous system. The immune system attacks and destroys myelin, the protective sheath that surrounds nerve cells. Scarring of the myelin impairs nerve function. Although the muscles are normal, they do not get the signals that trigger voluntary movement.

What is rhabdomyolysis and how is it treated?

Rhabdomyolysis is a disorder involving myoglobin. Myoglobin is an important protein in skeletal muscle. It binds oxygen and gives Type I muscle fibers their red color. When a skeletal muscle is damaged, some myoglobin is released into the bloodstream. It breaks down into toxic compounds that travel to the kidneys. If too many muscle fibers break down and dump large amounts of myoglobin into the bloodstream, the kidneys can sustain major damage. Also, large amounts of fluid can move from the bloodstream into dead muscle tissue. This reduces the fluid volume of the blood and reduces blood flow to the kidneys, causing even more damage. The result is the disease rhabdomyolysis.

Anything that damages skeletal muscle can cause the disease. It can result from severe exertion such as marathon running or from a trauma such as a car accident. Exposure to extreme heat or cold, a seizure, alcoholism, or a drug overdose can trigger it, as can some diseases of the circulatory system.

Its symptoms include red or dark brown urine, muscle tenderness and weakness, stiffness, and aching. Other symptoms may include seizures, joint pain, and extreme fatigue. The first step in treatment is hydration: getting enough water back into the body to increase blood volume and flush myoglobin from the kidneys. Medications help restore kidney function and stop the breakdown of myoglobin into toxic compounds.

Can muscles get cancer?

Yes, but rarely. Cancer is uncontrolled cell growth of any organ or tissue. Muscle cells do not normally divide at all, so it's unusual for them to begin dividing out of control. Nevertheless, tumors do sometimes develop in muscle tissue. Some are benign; they stay in one place and stop growing after a time. Others are malignant; their cells can travel to other organs and cause possible life-threatening cancers in other sites.

A leiomyoma is a benign tumor of smooth muscle. One can arise almost anywhere in the body in either men or women. The most common leiomyoma is a fibroid tumor that develops in a woman's uterus. It is actually a leiomyoma of the uterine muscle.

A leiomyosarcoma is a malignant tumor of involuntary muscle tissue. It often occurs in at the back of the abdomen near the kidneys. (The suffix *-sarcoma* denotes a malignant tumor that begins in the mesodermal or middle cell layer in the embryo, from which muscles, connective tissue, and bones develop.) A leiomyosarcoma can also form in the deep, soft tissues of the legs or arms, especially in the elderly.

Tumors of the skeletal muscle include rhabdomyoma and the malignant rhabdomyosarcoma. Rhabdomyoma usually develops in the chest, larynx, pharynx, or tongue. Men face a greater risk than women do, although the tumor is sometimes found in the hearts of infants. Rhabdomyosarcoma is rare. It most often appears in childhood. The site is usually the arms or legs—and less often, the head, neck, urinary bladder, or vagina. It is a fast-growing tumor. Other cancers that may occur in muscle include lipomas (fat), hemangiomas (blood vessels), myxomas (mesodermal tissue), and fibromas (fibrous tissue).

A Day in the Life of a Physical Therapist

. . . . .

*If the muscles aren't balanced, the joint will not work properly.
I don't mean balance like standing on your tiptoes. I mean
that your agonists and antagonists are working against
each other as they should.* [172]
—Shari Works, R.P.T.

. . . . .

Shari Works, physical therapist

*S*hari Works hates swelling.

"Some people say that swelling is part of the normal inflammation process, so let it go. But if it has been there for a long time, it is not helping," Works says—and she tries hard to get rid of it. She remembers a time when her efforts failed. She told a man with a swollen ankle to take "contrast baths." Bathe in hot water, then ice water, repeatedly, she told him, to get the swelling down. When he returned one week later, his ankle was still swollen. "Have you been taking the contrast baths?" she asked. "Every day," he affirmed. He described his method. He sat in the bathtub with his ankle elevated, well out of the water. He submerged the rest of his body in the hottest water his tap would provide. Then he drained the tub and filled it with cold water, calling for his wife to bring ice from the kitchen. Again he kept his swollen ankle high and dry. "He was giving himself a full body contrast bath but never treating his ankle," Works reports. "Can you imagine how uncomfortable he must have been?" Works responded in the only way she could. She suggested a wash pan for contrast baths of his ankle.

Works is a physical therapist. She sees patients of all ages with many different complaints, often involving severe pain. Her job is to relieve the pain and, at the same time, correct what's causing it. "A lot of physical therapy is looking at balancing all the muscles and the stresses and strains on every joint in your body," she says. "If somebody comes in with a low back problem, I look not only at the back, but also the hips, pelvis, upper back, diaphragm, upper trunk, and lower trunk. I look at everything, because everything is interrelated." Works uses ultrasound treatments, electrical stimulation, and massage to relieve pain. She manipulates joints and soft tissues to return them to their normal range of motion. To help achieve and maintain muscle balance, she shows her patients stretches and strengthening exercises they can do at home.

Works sees many teenagers who complain of pain in the upper back. The pain feels like a dagger between the shoulder blades, so her clients think the pain is coming from there. But the source is actually the muscles of the chest. Young people are slumping forward—shoulders rounded, back humped—in school, at the dinner table, and at their computers. The muscles of the spine and shoulder blades are being overworked, because the muscles in the front are constantly pulling them. The pain is a symptom of that overwork. To prevent such problems, Works reminds her patients to sit up straight. She recommends sitting on an exercise ball when working at the computer. Balancing on the ball requires keeping the back, shoulder, and chest in proper alignment. The result? No pain!

Other young people have—literally—a pain in the neck. It often comes from spending a lot of time working at a computer or driving a car. Its source is the sternocleidomastoid muscle that runs from the sternum and clavicle to the temporal bone of the head, behind the ear. Its action is to flex the neck and thrust it forward, but too much time spent in that position overworks it. The result is pain, not in the sternocleidomastoid itself, but in the muscles at the back of the neck that oppose it. Works offers her clients some tips on how to avoid neck pain. To get out of bed in

the morning, don't thrust the head forward and jerk straight up. That action strains the sternocleidomastoid. Instead, roll over onto one side and push up with the arms. No strain, no pain!

Works also treats many patients in their teens—often girls—who complain of shin splints. They feel pain along the shaft of the tibia, the long bone at the front of the lower leg. The pain's source is usually the peroneus muscles that run along the outer side of the lower leg. They are overworked because the gluteal muscles of the buttocks are weak. "The girls come in with weak gluteal muscles," Works says. "They are hanging on the shafts of their leg bones. They are not using the muscle dynamics in their legs to keep themselves upright." To ease the pain, Works shows girls how to stretch overtight hamstrings and the tendons that run down over the heels. She shows them how to strengthen the peroneus, the gluteal muscles, and the abductors, which are the major balancers for standing. She emphasizes strengthening the body's "core"—the abdomen and low back—with exercises such as leg lifts that tighten abdominal muscles.

Works finds that many of her young adult clients have poor muscle tone and little muscle strength. The main problems in the teen years, she believes, are bad nutrition and poor posture. Teens aren't eating the nutritious foods they need to build strong muscles and bones. They are filling up on soft drinks and sugar-loaded juices and eating too few dairy foods, vegetables, and whole grain foods. They are slumping while they watch TV, study, or play video games. The "cool" stance of belly protruding and back curved makes matters worse, she says.

So do exercise machines if they are used improperly. Too many teens fail to adjust them correctly and end up straining a muscle. Overzealous training can do harm too. "People think, 'the more the better,' but if you do not have the strength, you are going to end up compensating with something else," she says. A muscle can cause pain when it pushes on a nerve ending or changes the alignment of a joint. For example, if the muscles that rotate the hip are out of balance, movement can pull the ball part of the hip joint out of its socket. "It all comes down to balancing the system," Works says.

Works has been a practicing physical therapist for twenty years. She loves her job because of the help she can provide and the friendships she builds with her clients. "What feels good inside is that I educate people," she explains. "The ones who get better are those who attempt to help themselves. It's not that I make them feel better. It's that they take care of themselves and do what they can to have a better life." Works's approach is usually successful. Recently, a woman she scarcely recognized stopped her at the post office. The woman thanked Works for all her help. "I still do the exercises you taught me!" the woman related proudly. Later, back at her office, Works reviewed her files. She hadn't seen that patient in seven years!

CHAPTER FIVE

24
QUESTIONS

YOU'VE ALWAYS WONDERED ABOUT

The brain recalls just what the muscles grope for; no more, no less.[173]
—WILLIAM FAULKNER, *ABSALOM, ABSALOM!*

Does everyone have the same muscles?

For the major muscles, the answer is yes, but there are some inborn differences. For example, the psoas major in the abdominal wall helps hold and protect the organs inside the abdomen. It is also a flexor muscle for the hip. It originates at the ribs and inserts on the long bone of the upper leg, the femur. But some fibers of the psoas major may insert by a long tendon into a part of the pubic bone, forming the psoas minor. The psoas minor has no known function, and 40 percent of us don't have it.[174] The platysma muscle is another example. In some people, it covers the front of the neck completely. In others, it's thin and narrow. In some people, it is missing altogether.

What causes a tic?

A tic or twitch is an involuntary contraction of a skeletal muscle, often of an eyelid. It's usually harmless. It may occur once, several times, or repeatedly over a period of minutes or hours. The cause in most people is stress. When the stress is removed, the tic goes away. Stronger, longer-lasting, or more extreme spasms may be symptoms of a drug reaction, heat injury, alcohol withdrawal, a neurological disease, or a more serious muscular disorder. If trembling occurs in relaxed muscles or if a seizure accompanies your tic, see a doctor.

Why doesn't the heart muscle get tired?

The average adult heart weighs about 1.1 pounds (500 g). It beats 40 million times a year with enough force to lift its owner 100 miles (160 km) above the Earth. Even if it does not need to speed up for exercise, it pumps 1,400 gallons (5,300 liters) of blood each day. That's nearly 38 million gallons (150 million l) in a lifetime.[175] How can the heart achieve such remarkable feats without fatigue?

The simplest answer is that the heart obtains, processes, and uses energy very effectively. Even at rest, the heart muscle uses comparatively more oxygen than skeletal muscles do. It extracts as much as 80 percent of the oxygen carried by red blood cells in the coronary arteries that supply it. In comparison, most other tissues use only about 25 percent.[176]

What are heart muscle cells doing with all that oxygen? They're getting energy. Mitochondria, the cells' powerhouses, make up only about 1 to 2 percent of the mass of the average skeletal muscle cell, but they are about 30 percent of the mass of a heart muscle cell.[177] The result is a cardiac muscle cell that never lacks in its energy-generating capacity. What's more, the heart is extremely adaptable in its use of fuel sources. It can get its energy from glucose and glycogen, fatty acids, or even the excess lactic acid that skeletal muscles release into the blood stream during exercise.

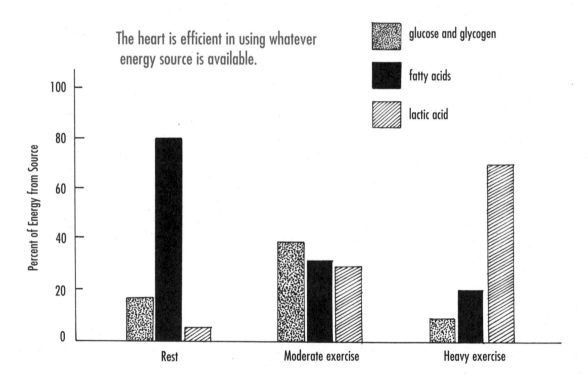

Redrawn from W.D. McArdle, F. I Katch, and V.L. Katch, *Exercise Physiology: Energy, Nutrition, and Human Performance*, Fifth Edition, (Philadelphia: Lippincott Williamson & Wilkins, 2001), p. 323.

If your ears remain stubbornly stationary, you are not alone. Only 10 percent of women and 20 percent of men can wiggle their ears naturally.[178] The ability may be inherited as a dominant characteristic—meaning if one of your parents can do it, you may have the talent too. The muscles that perform the action are the auricularis muscles, an apt name because *auricula* means *ear* in Latin. The muscles surround the ear: one in the front, one in the back, and one above. They are fastened to the bones and tissues of the scalp on one end and to the skin around the ear at the other. The same nerve that produces facial expressions, cranial nerve VII or the facial nerve, also stimulates these muscles to contract.

Physical therapist Shari Works says nonwigglers can learn to wiggle their ears, although the outcome might not be worth the effort. She says an electrical stimulus applied to the auricularis muscles will cause them to contract. By feeling the response, anyone could eventually learn to wiggle the ears at will.

As to why these (mostly) useless muscles are there in the first place, Canadian geneticist Ronald Davidson offers an answer. "Humans can use the same muscles

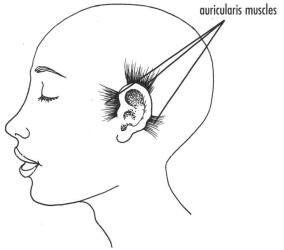

auricularis muscles

If you can move your auricularis muscles, you can wiggle your ears.

as rabbits, horses, and dogs to move their ears," he says. "They serve a purpose among animals in the wild to help localize the origin of sounds, some of which could signal danger." [179]

Is the penis a muscle, and is an erection a contraction?

The penis is not a muscle. Its shaft is made of spongy tissue packed with blood vessels. During sexual arousal (or sometimes for no apparent reason at all), blood collects in the penis. The spongy tissues fill with fluid, causing the penis to harden and rise. This is an erection. It has nothing to do with muscles and is neither a voluntary nor an involuntary muscle action.

However, smooth muscle does play a role in the maturation of sperm, the maintenance of an erection, and the propulsion of sperm from the body when a man ejaculates. Inside the testicles, sperm form in tiny tubules. Three or four layers of smooth muscle cells surround the tubules.[180] Immature sperm move from the tubules into a larger tube, the epididymis, where they mature. Peristaltic contractions of smooth muscle cells surrounding the epididymis move the sperm through it. A muscle called the ischiocavernosus runs beneath the base of the penis at its sides. It helps maintain an erection. So does the bulbospongiosus muscle, which encircles the penis below skin level. Mature sperm are stored at the end of the epididymis. The muscle fibers there do not contract spontaneously. At ejaculation, they contract at the same time that the muscles of the vas deferens contract. The vas deferens is the tube that carries the sperm to the urethra, where it is expelled during ejaculation.

What causes hiccups?

The trouble begins in the diaphragm, the major muscle of breathing. Normally, it drops when you inhale and rises when you exhale. But if it starts contracting when it shouldn't, the vocal folds of the larynx close. They stop air from flowing in and produce the distinctive, popping sound of the hiccup. Stomach irritation can cause hiccups, but they often happen for no apparent reason and disappear just as quickly as they came. You can usually stop hiccups by holding your breath, breathing repeatedly into a paper bag, drinking a glass of cold water, or eating a teaspoon of sugar.

Seek medical help for hiccups that last longer than 48 hours. A healthcare provider may massage the carotid sinus in the neck (do NOT attempt this at home) or flush the stomach with water or a salt solution. (Do not attempt either of these procedures yourself!) If hiccups continue, prescription drugs or a tube inserted into the nose and running to the stomach may provide relief.

What's the record for nonstop hiccups? More than 60 years.[181]

Why can't we all be Olympic athletes?

There are as many reasons as there are competitive sports, but the genes we are born with make a big difference. One study in rats proves the point. Researchers at the Medical College of Ohio in Toledo bred two strains of rats. The "high-capacity" rats could run four times as long as their "low-capacity" cousins before reaching exhaustion. When the researchers studied the animals' hearts, they found that the high-capacity animals had a 49 percent greater heart output. The difference was due to stroke volume, the amount of blood pumped by a single contraction of the heart muscle.[182]

Heart action isn't the only inherited difference. Skeletal muscle fiber types vary too. While many other animals have individual muscles that are made mainly of fast cells or slow cells only, most human muscles are a mixture of cell types. "We do not have any muscles that are purely fast or slow," says University of Calgary biologist Douglas Syme. It is not known why. Different people have different degrees of "fastness" or "slowness" in many of their muscles. For example, Olympic sprinters have a high proportion of fast cells in their leg muscles. "I—and I expect you—can never be an Olympic sprinter," Syme says, "no matter how much we train, because we just weren't born with the right kind of muscle."[183]

No matter what we are born with, however, we can all improve with exercise in pursuit of our personal best. Greek scientists studied nine pairs of identical twins, all boys, ages 11 to 14. Because they were genetically identical, the boys all inherited the same bodily characteristics. They all started the study with the same level of physical fitness. Then one boy of each pair ran three times a week for six months, while the other twin made no changes in his level of physical activity. At the end of the study, the trained twins had increased their maximal oxygen consumption by nearly 11 percent. The trained twins had reduced their body fat from 17.8 to 16.2 percent.[184]

Does muscle weigh more than fat?

For an equal volume, yes. Muscle is denser than fat so, for amounts that occupy equal amounts of space, muscle weighs more. The reason is that muscle is as much as 80 percent water. Fat tissue contains hardly any water. The difference in density explains why very lean people find floating a challenge, while people with a higher percentage of body fat float with ease. Lean people are denser—heavier for their size—so they tend to sink. The density difference also explains why you can lose fat but gain weight. Exercising can reduce body fat, while at the same time increasing muscle mass. The result may be a weight gain.

Can muscle turn to fat?

No. Muscle cells are muscle cells, and fat cells are fat cells. One type does not change to the other. When we say that a formerly muscular athlete has "gone to fat," we mean that the person has reduced or stopped training while still eating as much or more. As a result, muscle mass has been lost, and fat mass has been gained.

Will I lose muscle as I get older?

With every passing year, the average person loses some muscle mass—and along with it some strength. The process is called sarcopenia. The word means "vanishing flesh." Most of the loss is in Type II (fast-twitch, anaerobic) muscle fibers.[185] The decline begins early in adult life. After age 30, thigh muscles shrink, muscle density declines, and the storage of fat within the muscle increases.[186] By age 40, strength is lost, first in the extensor muscles of the forearm and the flexors of the lower leg.[187] Between ages 50 and 70, strength drops by 30 percent. Muscle strength declines by about 15 percent per decade in the sixth and seventh decades of life and by about 30 percent after that.[188]

Many factors contribute to sarcopenia. The manufacture of proteins in muscle cells declines with age.[189] Researchers also find higher levels of chemical factors made by the immune system and lower levels of growth hormones in the blood of elderly people. Other chemicals—not in blood, but in muscle cells themselves—may also be involved. Researchers at the Mayo Clinic studied muscle samples from healthy men and women ranging in age from 18 to 89. They found less DNA in the mitochondria in the muscle cells of older people. Mitochondrial DNA was more damaged in the elderly too.[190]

While sarcopenia seems (at least for now) an unavoidable part of aging, there are ways to fight back. One way is diet. Older people may need more protein in their diets. Some can benefit from taking amino acid supplements.[191] Another way is exercise. Aerobic activities that get the heart pumping faster—such as dancing and swimming—speed up muscle growth in people of any age.[192] Resistance exercises help people retain muscle too. Older people who have lifted weights for 15 to 20 years have muscles the same size as a sedentary twenty-year-old.[193]

Why do people gesture when they talk?

Part of the reason is cultural. We learn to "talk with our hands," and it's good that we do. In one study, researchers at the University of Chicago asked people to explain math problems and remember a list of items at the same time. The scientists found that people who were allowed to gesture as they explained the math remembered 20 percent more items from the list.[194] In another study, psychologist Spencer

Kelly at Colgate University showed college students videos of professors lecturing. Some saw the professor gesturing during a lecture. Others watched an edited version, without the gestures. The students who saw the gestures said they liked the professor more and thought they understood the lecture better.[195]

What happens to muscles during sleep?

Not all sleep is the same. Sleep occurs in stages that repeat in cycles throughout the night. During some of the lighter stages, the major muscles of the body move frequently, causing the individual to change position, on average, some thirty to fifty times a night.[196]

But the REM (rapid eye movement) sleep stage is different. In REM, the only muscles that continue to work are the heart, diaphragm, eyes, and the smooth muscles of the blood vessels and internal organs. The major muscles keep their tone, but they do not move. The body is almost completely paralyzed.

Normally, our sleeping brains aren't aware of—or concerned about—the immobility. When we become aware that our muscles aren't responding—usually during the transition time between REM sleep and waking—we experience "sleep paralysis," or the feeling of being immobilized in bed, unable to call for help. About half of us experience sleep paralysis once or twice in our lifetimes. Perhaps as many as 6 percent of us have frequent episodes.[197] In most cases, sleep paralysis passes and is forgotten. Some people, however, experience hallucinations and fear. In such cases, it's wise to seek medical help.

Strange as it may seem, the answer is yes. When you contract a muscle for a long time, force begins to diminish as the muscle grows fatigued. To recruit more motor units to the task, the brain sends signals that step up activation.[198] That increased signal travels to both limbs, whether both are in use or not. The process is called cross-transfer. It can help people who have had both short-term and long-term injuries. For example, if your left leg is in a cast, you can "exercise it" by doing calf raises, leg extensions, and hamstring curls with your right leg. "By working the opposite leg, you can decrease the amount of atrophy [loss of muscle mass] that you'll get in the casted limb," says Nick DiNubile, team doctor for the Philadelphia 76ers basketball team and the Pennsylvania Ballet.[199]

For people who are paralyzed, this fact offers an option for some measure of rehabilitation. Neurologists in Los Angeles recorded electrical activity in the leg muscles of patients who had suffered a complete spinal cord injury. The patients could not move either leg voluntarily. But when therapists supported the patients and worked one leg through a stepping motion, the muscles of the nonmoving leg responded with some electrical activity. "The human spinal cord can use sensory information about [the opposite limb] to increase muscle activation, even when there is no limb movement," the researchers concluded.[200]

It's a well-known training technique: imagine yourself clearing the high jump bar, doing a perfect swan dive, or topping hurdles at a record pace. Surprise! Surprise! Your time and technique seem to improve. Are we fooling ourselves, or is imagination an effective training regimen? To find out, researchers at the Cleveland Clinic recruited thirty healthy, young volunteers to participate in an experiment. They divided them into three groups. People in the first group imagined moving their little fingers. Those in the second group actually performed the movement. People in the control group did nothing at all. Those who exercised increased muscle strength by 53 percent compared to the controls. Those who only imagined the exercise increased their strength by 35 percent. The scientists explain the result as a function of brain activity. Imagining the movement "trained and enabled the brain to generate stronger signals to muscle."[201]

Am I too big (or too small) for a certain sport?

It comes as no surprise that tall people have an advantage in basketball, while jockeys need to be short and light. The small and light excel in gymnastics too, but it takes poundage to survive as an NFL lineman. But are there ideal sizes and shapes for other sports? In his book *Muscle Physiology and Cardiac Function*, University of Indiana professor Lincoln Ford reports that average heights (more or less) dominate among top competitors in most sports. In boxing, it pays to be short. Tall boxers have a longer reach and greater power in their punch, but they're slower. In track, shorter runners have a slight advantage in sprinting and long-distance running. Taller runners do better in the middle distances.[202]

To work out the math of height and athletic performance, Ford teamed up with Chinese scientists to assess champion weightlifters. They found that the maximum weight a lifter could heft was proportional to the lifter's height squared (height multiplied by height).

Height is a good predictor of weightlifting ability.

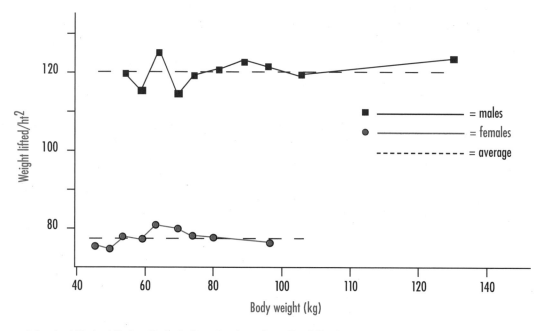

Redrawn from L.E. Ford et al, "Gender and Height-related Limits of Muscle Strength in World Weightlifting Champions," *Journal of Applied Physiology* (September 2000), p. 1062.

Muscle mass was proportional to height cubed (height times height times height). Height predicted the cross-sectional area of the major muscles. The reason, the researchers think, has to do with growth and development. Individual muscle cells achieve an upper limit that cannot be increased with additional training. At that point, it's the *number* of cells that determines power, and that number is determined by bone length.[203]

If there is an "ideal sport" for most people, Ford claims it's soccer. It accommodates the widest range of sizes and body shapes.

Why do men have bigger muscles than women?

Testosterone. Both men and women have this hormone in their blood, but men make a lot more of it. The testicles manufacture it. Some men have higher levels than others do. Testosterone increases the rate of muscle synthesis. In one study, men who had low levels of testosterone got replacement doses for six months. Their rate of muscle protein synthesis increased by 56 percent. Their muscle mass rose by an average of 20 percent.[204]

If you are thinking that testosterone might be a good way for average people to grow bigger muscles, think again. Testosterone "masculinizes" women. It causes them to grow unwanted hair, get deeper voices, and change their body shape. Too much testosterone in men elevates the risk of prostate cancer.

Do men's and women's muscles differ?

Yes, and it's a mixed bag of differences. Women have advantages in some areas, while men take the lead in others.

Women have almost twice the endurance of men when performing the same exercises.[205] University of Colorado and Marquette University scientists matched men and women for strength. The researchers compared the endurance times, or "fatigability," of their subjects during isometric contractions of the elbow flexor muscles. In one task, the subjects held an arm rigid for as long as possible. In another, they held an arm rigid with a weight attached to the wrist. The force the men and women produced was the same, but the time to task failure was longer for women. Men had the same motivation to succeed as women, and no differences in the action of the nervous system were found. The researchers concluded that a difference in muscle activity produced greater endurance in women. The source of that difference is unknown.[206]

Men outdo women on muscle strength most of the time. That's no surprise, given the muscle-promoting effects of testosterone. But evidence suggests that women may be able to increase their strength more than they might think. University of Massachusetts researchers measured muscle size and strength changes in men and women who participated in resistance training programs. Men increased their muscle size a little more than women did, but the women outpaced the men in their strength gains. They didn't get stronger than the men, but they improved their strength more.[207]

Scientists can't reach an agreement about the response of the sexes to damage-inducing exercise. In animals other than humans, it's clear that the same amount of exercise causes less damage in females than in males. However, studies on humans show mixed results. Some conclude there is no difference between men and women. Others find that women sustain greater exercise-induced muscle damage than men do.[208]

There's a downside for women. Then tend to develop muscular and skeletal problems of the wrist, neck, and shoulder. The traditional view was that women develop upper body problems because they often do close, detailed, repetitive work. But Ohio State University scientists found otherwise. Even when they do the same jobs as men, women face a greater risk of disorders such as carpal tunnel syndrome (pain in the wrist when a nerve is compressed). The reason is not known, but it's probably a combination of social and biological factors.[209]

Can muscle be transplanted?

As long as a blood supply can be established to keep muscle and tendon alive, muscle can be transplanted. Doctors often perform the surgery after injury or nerve damage destroys a muscle. Muscle transplants can help people with cerebral palsy or polio. The transplanted muscle needs to be one that has a similar size, shape, and function to the one it replaces. If the muscle transplant uses the patient's own muscles, it's called an autograft. The immune system does not reject autografts. The body recognizes the proteins of the transplanted tissues as "self."

If transplanted muscle comes from an organ donor, it's called an allograft. For allografts, proteins must be typed and matched as much as possible to diminish chances of rejection by the immune system. Any allograft requires the patient to take immune-suppressing drugs to reduce the risk of rejection. Because suppressing the immune system diminished a person's ability to fight off infections and diseases, muscle transplants are performed only in special cases. For example, a man who was already on immune-suppressing drugs from a kidney transplant lost a part of his scalp to skin cancer. Transplanted skin and muscle from an organ donor restored the lost tissue in the first successful muscle allograft.[210]

A different approach is to transplant not whole muscles, but muscle cells. For example, in 2003, a U.S. research team reported transplanting muscle cells in three patients who were waiting for heart transplants. The source of the transplanted cells was the patients' thighs. The skeletal muscle cells from their thighs were injected into their damaged hearts. After the patients had heart transplants, researchers examined their old hearts for signs of new cell growth. They found that injected cells survived in the hearts. New muscle fibers began forming, as did new blood vessels. Because the source of the cells was each patient's own body, there was no rejection by the immune system.[211] "These results give us the first indication that muscle cell transplants, even from an entirely different kind of muscle, could one day be used to repair damaged, failing hearts without danger of rejection," says University of Michigan cardiac surgeon Francis Pagani.[212]

What's a tendon transfer?

In tendon transfer surgery, surgeons cut a tendon and reposition it so the muscle attached to it performs a different function. Doctors use the procedure to treat several different kinds of injury or disability, including functions lost to stroke or arthritis. Also, people who have experienced spinal cord injuries may lose the use of some, but not all, muscles in an arm. A tendon transfer can recruit a functional muscle to restore the ability to move the elbow, wrist, hand, or a finger.

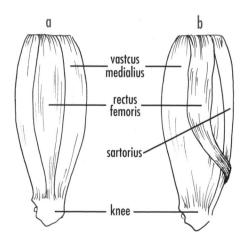

A tendon transfer can help some people with cerebral palsy bend their knees better when they walk. Shown here are front views of a patient's right thigh (a) before surgery and (b) after a tendon transfer of the rectus femoris to the sartorius.

Redrawn from D.S. Asakawa et al, "Three-Dimensional Muscle-Tendon Geometry After Rectus Femoris Tendon Transfer," *The Journal of Bone and Joint Surgery* (American), (February 2004), p. 351.

Is it possible to grow muscle outside the body?

Yes, and scientists are developing new and better ways to do it. In 2005 U.S. researchers reported using a fibrin gel as a base medium for growing myoblasts. (Fibrin is a protein normally found in blood. Myoblasts are a type of stem cell. Stem cells are undifferentiated—that is, they are not specialized as any particular type of cells. Under the right conditions, myoblasts can develop into muscle fibers.) Three weeks after the researchers put the cells on the gel, they tested the contracting ability of the muscle fibers that had grown there. The cells were normal, and they generated a contracting force in the normal range. They also responded to growth hormone just as muscle cells in the body do.[213]

That same year, a team of Israeli and U.S. researchers grew new muscle in the laboratory. The muscle was complete with its own network of blood vessels. First, they seeded a sponge-like, three-dimensional plastic scaffold with myoblasts and endothelial cells, which are the precursors to mature skeletal muscle and blood vessel cells. They also added connective tissue cells called fibroblasts to the mix. The cells quickly organized into tissue on the scaffold. The myoblasts elongated and aligned themselves into muscle fibers. The fibroblasts cells boosted the growth of endothelial cells into a network of blood vessels. Then the researchers successfully transplanted the new muscle tissue into living mice. The transplanted muscle tissue grew and developed within the mice's bodies.[214] In the future, a sample of a person's own cells might be used as the source of "seed" cells. "The idea is that this hopefully will be used to repair or replace damaged muscle tissue when needed," says team leader Shulamit Levenberg.[215] People who suffer muscle loss from burns, injuries, or disease could benefit.

Can stem cells repair damaged heart muscle?

Maybe, but scientists haven't yet perfected the technique. In 2001 U.S. researchers injected stem cells from the bone marrow of mice into the animals' damaged hearts. Later, they found evidence that the stem cells had developed into cardiac muscle cells.[216] Since cardiac muscle does not naturally repair itself, this was big news. The technique offered hope for human heart patients.

In the years that followed, doctors tried transplanting stem cells from bone marrow into the hearts of people who had suffered heart attacks. Nearly all the trials showed positive results. Many bedridden patients returned to their normal activities. But the improvements were, on average, only 5 to 10 percent, and some studies have called into question whether cardiac muscle cells are actually growing from the stem cells.[217] Many researchers think that stem cells cause blood vessels—not heart muscle—to develop. Others think that some side effect of the treatment—perhaps the release of chemical clues such as growth factors—may account for the improvements.[218]

Whatever the cause, research continues. New findings offer hope for repairing heart attack damage with stem cells. In 2005 scientists at Johns Hopkins University in Baltimore studied 14 pigs whose hearts were damaged by heart attacks. Seven of the pigs received between 12 and 15 microscopic injections of adult stem cells taken from their own bone marrow. Each injection contained nearly 200 million cells. The other seven pigs, the control group, got no stem cells. In the stem-cell pigs, the researchers found a 50–75 percent restoration of the heart muscle's structure and function in only two months. The control group developed heart failure in that same time.[219] The scientists are continuing their work. They are trying to find out how and why the adult stem cells developed into new, healthy heart tissue and how long the healing effects will last.

Are there
artificial
muscles?

When you think artificial muscle, say electroactive polymer, or EAP for short. An EAP is a plastic that changes shape in response to an electric current or a chemical change. The concept is simple. Robotics expert Yoseph Bar-Cohen of NASA's Jet Propulsion Laboratory explains: "If you take two metal plates and put rubber between them and drive one plate with positive charge, the other plate with negative charge, they will be attracted to each other and they will squeeze whatever is between them."[220] From that simple principle, researchers are working to develop polymers—and means of activating them—that can mimic the action of real muscles. One application would be to improve prostheses for people who have lost limbs. "My vision is that we may see one day either bionic people, namely individuals with artificial muscles, or robots that mimic biology," Bar-Cohen says.[221]

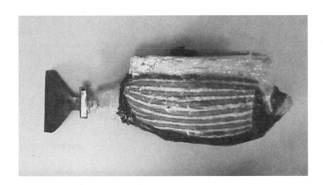

This robotic fish swims under the power of the artificial muscle in its tail. Using 2 volts of electricity, it moves at a maximum speed of 6 feet (2 meters) a minute.

EAP research follows two basic lines. Some polymers expand and contract in response to an electric current. Others—which work more like living muscle—respond to a chemical change. In the 1980s, researchers at MIT reported on the collapse of certain polymer gels in an electric field.[222] A voltage gradient through them forces fixed and moveable charged particles to redistribute themselves. The result is a change in shape, from a flat sheet to a curved structure, not too different from a contracting muscle.

Newer materials made of polymers combined with metals change shape in an electrical field. They also work in reverse. Changing their shape generates an electrical field.[223] That property suggests another possible use for artificial muscle. The polymers made into fibers and implanted in clothing might provide electricity the wearer needs to run electronic gadgets such as computers or CD players. No more batteries!

To stimulate research on artificial muscles, Bar-Cohen issued in 1999 a challenge to researchers worldwide: Develop a robotic arm powered by artificial muscle that can win an arm-wrestling contest with a human. Six years later, the first competition took place, with three competitors matched against 17-year-old high school student Panna Felson from San Diego. The artificial muscles were of both types, two powered electrically and one chemically triggered. Panna— who was chosen for her interest in robotics, not her arm strength— beat the best of her competitors in only 26 seconds.[224] Still, the competition was a milestone on the road toward developing a functional, artificial muscle. The Wright brothers' first airplane flight lasted only 12 seconds, Bar-Cohen reminds us.

Can muscles move after death?

Nearly 40 percent of patients who show no electrical activity of the brain have spontaneous movement of their muscles, such as jerking the fingers or bending the toes. "The living cells that [order] these muscles to move [are] not brain cells or brain stem cells, but cells located in the spinal cord," says Spanish neurologist Joan Marti-Fabregas.[225] Because a diagnosis of "brain death" can prompt a decision to remove life-support machines, such movements can be distressing for family members who interpret them as signs of life. A delay, however, can interfere with a patient's or family's desire to donate organs for transplant. The movements are seen in the first 24 hours after a diagnosis of brain death, but never after 72 hours.[226] "We found that these movements are more common than has been reported or believed," says Buenos Aries neurologist Jose Bueri. "People need to know that these movements are spinal reflexes that do not involve any brain activity."[227]

What causes rigor mortis?

Rigor mortis is the rigid state of all muscle fibers after death. To understand it, we must first understand why muscles get tired. "Our muscles get tired very fast if we push or pull for a long time, even if we don't actually move anything," says University of Calgary zoologist Douglas Syme.[228] "That is because even though our muscles aren't shortening, the nerves are still turning them on and off, and the crossbridges are still pulling and letting go, all of which costs energy. However, some animals, such as clams and mussels, must hold their shells tightly shut for long periods of time (when the tide is out, or when a raccoon or seastar is trying to pry them open). Why don't they get tired? They have developed a remarkable mechanism called 'catch,' which allows them to lock their crossbridges tight. Hardly any energy is used and the muscle cannot be stretched."[229]

There is one short period of time in which human muscles also enter a state much like catch, becoming rigid and inflexible, but not using any energy. It is called rigor mortis, which means "rigid death." It is not a contraction of muscles after death, but a locking of the muscles in position. "We do not fully understand how 'catch' works, but catch and rigor mortis share a similar outcome by somehow causing the crossbridges to lock in place," Syme says.[230] In life, muscles contract when a nerve impulse triggers the release of calcium in the muscle fibers. The crossbridges then begin their cycles of attachment, pulling, and detachment (when the crossbridges let go). The contraction ends when calcium is picked up and put back into storage. All the crossbridges soon end up detached and unable to reattach, so the muscle relaxes. Both of these processes—crossbridge detachment and getting rid of calcium—require energy in the form of ATP. After death, cells no longer make ATP, so the crossbridges stay in place and the muscle gets stiff.

If the place of death is not too hot or too cold, signs of rigor mortis appear within two to four hours. The body reaches its maximum stiffness in about 6 to 12 hours. Rigor disappears between 18 and 36 hours after death. That happens because muscle proteins start to break down. As they do, the crossbridges between actin and myosin collapse, and muscles relax.

Muscles in Space

It's human nature to stretch, to go, to see, to understand.
Exploration is not a choice, really; it's an imperative.[231]
—MICHAEL COLLINS, ASTRONAUT

$\mathcal{E}$ ven before Russian cosmonaut Yuri Gagarin became the first human to orbit the Earth in 1961, those who would travel in space—and those who would send them there—have wondered how the reduced gravity of space would affect the human body. The problem is obvious. Normal human cells, tissues, and organs have adapted over millions of years to work in Earth's gravity. How, then, will their structure and function change when gravity shrinks to a fraction of its Earth-norm, as it does during Earth orbit or travel between planets?

Since the 1960s, manned space flights have provided part of the answer. Microgravity affects all body systems. Blood and body fluids migrate from the legs upward, causing the faces of astronauts to grow puffy. Astronauts can measure as much as 2 inches (5 cm) or more taller in space than they are on Earth.[232] They assume a bent, forward-curled posture to maintain their balance in microgravity. Shifts in fluid can redden their eyes, make their noses run, and give them headaches and nausea. Blood volume diminishes and circulation is impaired. Astronauts often experience space motion sickness, a disorder not unlike seasickness. Long-term effects of living and working in space may include bone loss, kidney failure, changes in blood pressure and heart rate, and an increased susceptibility to infectious diseases.

Another major effect is a loss of muscle mass, strength, and endurance. "Even with onboard exercise, astronauts face the risk of losing muscle mass and function because their muscles are not bearing enough weight, or load," says space scientist Vincent Caiozzo.[233] "Weightlessness reduces strength and mass and increases fatigue in the skeletal muscles of the limbs, especially in anti-gravity muscles such as the soleus."[234] (As you may recall, the soleus is one of the muscles in the leg that lets you point your toe. You use it with every step you take.) The reason is biochemical. Because the muscles bear less weight, they make less protein. The contractile proteins in muscle fibers are lost more than other proteins. More of the actin thin filaments are lost than of the myosin thick filaments.

Researchers think these losses explain why the force that muscle fibers produce is less after spaceflight than before. They may also explain postflight increases in the maximal velocity of shortening of muscle fibers. The proportion of Type II, fast-twitch fibers increases during space flights, even during relatively short flights of fewer than two weeks.[235] These changes can affect astronauts during their space missions. "Spaceflight-deconditioned crewmembers may be less able to complete strenuous tasks, such as extravehicular activity of postflight emergency egress from the Space Shuttle, or may be at increased risk for injury during or after space-flight," NASA scientists say.[236]

These findings beg the question: *How can the loss of muscle mass be prevented?* To probe that question in Earth-based studies, researchers sometimes ask healthy volunteers to stay in bed for days or weeks. "One cause of muscle atrophy in space is lack of muscular activity," says physician Arny Ferrando. "That's

Space travel reduces the power and force of Type I and Type II muscle fibers in the soleus (leg) muscle of astronauts.

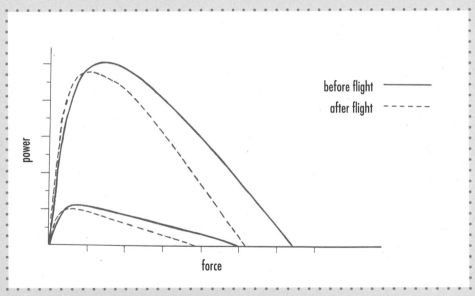

Redrawn from R.H. Fitts, D.R. Riley, and J.J. Widrick, "Physiology of a Microgravity Environment: Invited Review: Microgravity and Skeletal Muscle," *Journal of Applied Physiology* (August 2000), pp. 823-839.

why bed rest is a good model because it minimizes activity, and like astronauts, you lose muscle mass primarily in the legs. When muscles are inactive, as they are in space, they don't make new proteins. If muscle breakdown rates are the same, that means you lose muscle."[237]

To conduct bed rest studies, investigators match subjects for age, sex, fitness levels, and other variables. Then they divide the volunteers into two groups. One group rests in bed without exercise. The other group also rests in bed but performs an exercise program. After a time, both groups are measured for strength, power, muscle response time, or other variables. In one such study, the no-exercise group lost 17 percent of whole muscle size and 40 percent of strength from one of their thigh muscles, the vastus lateralis, during seven weeks of bed rest. Members of the exercise group who performed four sets of squatting exercises every three days maintained that muscle's size and strength.[238]

From such studies, researchers have concluded that high-resistance exercise (for example, working against stiff rubber bands) may reduce, if not prevent, the loss of muscle mass that astronauts experience.[239] However, the problem is far from solved. Many exercise programs that have been tried in space have failed to provide as much protection against muscle (and bone) loss as

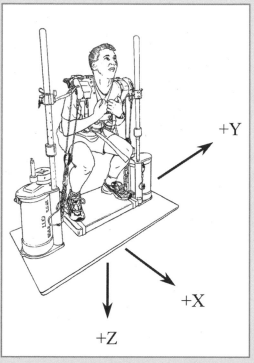

An astronaut performs squat exercises on the International Space Station's iRED.

Reprinted with permission from: Lee SMC, Cobb K, Loehr JA, Nguyen D, Schneider SM. "Foot-ground reaction force during resistive exercise in parabolic flight." Aviat Space Environ Med 2004; 75: 405–12.

researchers had hoped for. It's hard to make high-resistance exercise devices work in microgravity; and determining whether devices such as the iRED (interim Resistive Exercise Device) in use on the International Space Station (ISS) can be effective will require years of research.[240]

"Spaceflight is a unique environment that poses several physiological challenges to the human body," said Scott Trappe, director of the Human Performance Laboratory at Ball State University in Muncie, Indiana. "As the various space agencies around the world focus their attention on long duration stays on the International Space Station, implementation of effective exercise regimens is essential for the health and well being of the crew members."[241]

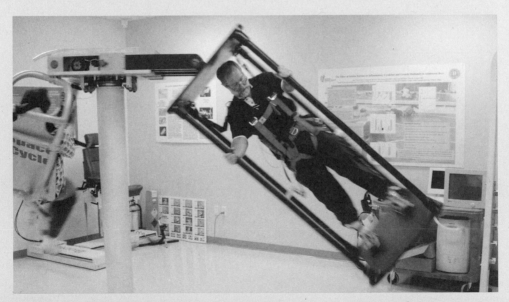

Space Cycle is an artificial gravity exercise gym that enables the rider to perform resistance-training exercises without the use of weights. To achieve the desired amount of force, the rider on the left powers the cycle while the rider on the right performs squats.

IN CLOSING

MORE QUESTIONS
THAN ANSWERS

The brain is like a muscle. When it is in use we feel very good.
Understanding is joyous.[242]

—CARL SAGAN

What have you thought about as you've read the questions and answers on these pages? Perhaps you have been struck by how complex an apparently simple thing like movement actually is. Your muscles are fundamental to your survival. Yet if you are like most people, you scarcely give them a thought. We have learned so much in the past 300-plus years, since Jan Swammerdam showed that animal spirits don't inflate muscles like balloons.

Three hundred years seems a long time to us, but it's a short time in human history. In fact, the view that Swammerdam challenged went unquestioned for 1,500 years before he lived and worked. Who's to say what scientists in another 1,500 years will say about our current understandings? Perhaps our ideas will seem as primitive to them as the notion of animal spirits seems to us.

Still, that's how science works. Old ideas explain a lot, but never enough when new observations are made. Then investigators who strive to understand the physical world revise their explanations and design new experiments to test them. More questions are asked, and more answers are found. New ideas replace old, and they, too, hold up for a while, until still more challenges are made. That process of explaining, testing, and finding new explanations will never end, so long as human beings seek to comprehend their minds, their bodies, and their universe. With each passing year, our eyes, our instruments, and our experiments tell us a little more, but every answer raises new questions. No matter how far we have come in understanding, we still have a long way to go. What you have read on these pages is only the beginning. Keep reading, keep learning, and keep asking questions. That's what powers the movement of mind and thought. It requires no muscle, but it's hard work anyway.

GLOSSARY

A band: A dark band that can be seen with a microscope. An A band is formed by aligned myosin filaments in a sarcomere. It causes the striations, or striping, of skeletal muscles.

Abdominal muscles: The muscles that form the supporting wall for the organs of the abdomen and pelvic regions.

Acetylcholine: A neurotransmitter that carries messages from nerve cells to muscles at the neuromuscular junction.

Actin: The thin-filament contractive protein in the sarcomere.

Adenosine triphosphate (ATP): The main energy-providing molecule in muscle cells.

Aerobic: Requiring oxygen.

Agonist: A muscle that produces a specific movement. See also *Antagonist.*

Anabolic steroid: A form of the male hormone testosterone. Anabolic steroids increase muscle mass. They are banned in most sports.

Anaerobic: Not requiring oxygen.

Antagonist: A muscle that opposes a specific motion, thus moving the joint opposite to the movement produced by an agonist.

Aponeurosis: A fibrous sheet or expanded tendon that serves as a muscle's attachment to other structures (such as the skeleton) at its origin or insertion.

ATP: See *Adenosine triphosphate.*

Atrophy: A loss of muscle mass.

Autoimmune disorder: A disorder caused by an attack of the immune system on the body's healthy cells, tissues, or organs.

Cardiac muscle: Heart muscle. Striated but involuntary.

Concentric: A muscle contraction in which the muscle shortens.

Congenital myasthenia: An inherited disease of muscle present at birth resulting from an abnormality of the neuromuscular junction.

Cramp: An involuntary muscle contraction that lasts and hurts.

Crossbridge: The temporary linkage between actin and the head of a myosin molecule when a muscle contracts.

DOMS: Delayed onset muscular soreness. Soreness felt 12 to 48 hours after exercise.

Eccentric: A muscle contraction in which the muscle lengthens.

Extensor: A muscle that increases the angle at a joint. For example, the quadriceps extend the knee (straighten it).

Fast twitch: A type of muscle fiber that produces brief bursts of power and speed. Fast-twitch muscle fibers are also called Type II fibers.

Filament: One of the contractile proteins of the muscle (actin or myosin).

Flexibility: The ability to move a specific joint and its corresponding muscle groups through the full, normal range of motion.

Flexor: A muscle that decreases the angle at a joint. For example, the hamstrings flex the knee (bend it).

"Floppy baby syndrome": A disorder in newborns and infants in which the muscles have too little tone.

Gene therapy: Any of several methods used to alter or replace genes in cells in order to treat a disorder.

Hamstrings: Large muscles at the back of the thigh that flex the knee.

Hernia: A condition in which part of the intestine pokes through a hole in the muscles of the abdominal wall.

Hypertrophy: An increase in the mass of a muscle.

I band: A band of actin filaments in a muscle that looks pale under a light microscope.

Immune system: The series of responses by which the body resists infection by microbes such as bacteria or viruses and rejects transplanted tissues or organs. The immune system also fights some cancers.

Inflammation: Swelling, redness, and pain often associated with the buildup of immune cells and substances around damaged tissue.

Insertion: The point of a skeletal muscle's attachment to the body that is farther from the center of the body than its other point of attachment, the origin.

Isometric: The type of muscle contraction that generates force, but muscle length does not change and no movement occurs. (Example: pushing against a wall.)

Larynx: Voice box.

Ligament: A strong fiber that holds bones together at the joints.

Marathon: A foot race covering 26.2 miles.

Mitochondria: The "power plants" of a muscle cell. Mitochondria make fresh supplies of ATP, the main energy-providing molecule in muscle cells. The singular term is *mitochondrion.*

Motor neuron: A specialized nerve cell that sends signals to a muscle fiber.

Motor unit: The group of muscle cells that is activated by a single motor neuron.

Muscle fatigue: The decline in a muscle's ability to function as expected following prolonged contraction.

Muscle fiber: An individual muscle cell. See also *Myocyte.*

Muscle spasm: A persistent contraction of muscle that cannot be stopped voluntarily. See also *Cramp.*

Muscle tone: The natural stiffness or tension in a resting muscle.

Muscular dystrophy: Any of a number of diseases that cause skeletal muscles to weaken and degenerate.

Myasthenia gravis: A chronic, progressive disease of muscular weakness caused by a defect at the neuromuscular junction.

Myoblast: An unspecialized cell that can develop into a muscle cell.

Myocyte: An individual muscle cell. See also *Muscle fiber.*

Myofibril: Contractile element of a muscle cell, consisting of a chain of sarcomeres.

Myoglobin: The oxygen-carrying, red-colored pigment in muscle fibers.

Myokine: A substance made and released by a muscle that affects some other organ in the body.

Myopathy: Any disorder of muscle that is not related to nerves.

Myosin: The thick-filament contractile protein in the sarcomere.

Myositis: Inflammation of a muscle.

Myostatin: A protein that regulates muscle growth. When the level of myostatin reaches a certain threshold value, muscle growth ceases.

Neuromuscular junction: The site where a neuron and muscle meet.

Neuron: A nerve cell.

Neurotransmitter: A substance that carries a message between neurons or from neurons to other kinds of cells.

Origin: The point of a skeletal muscle's attachment to the body that is closer to the midline of the body that is its other point of attachment, the insertion.

Peristalsis: The automatic, involuntary, slow contraction of muscles in the digestive tract.

Pharynx: Throat.

Quadriceps: The muscles on the front of the thigh that extend (straighten) the knee.

Referred pain: Pain felt at a site other than its cause.

Reflex: An involuntary reaction to a stimulus.

Rhabdomyolysis: A serious disease involving breakdown of skeletal muscle fibers and release of myoglobin into the bloodstream.

Rigor mortis: The rigid state of all muscle fibers after death.

Rotator cuff: Four muscles and their associated tendons that connect muscles of the shoulder blade to the upper arm bone.

Sarcolemma: The plasma membrane of a muscle cell.

Sarcomere: The smallest functional unit of a muscle cell, consisting of actin and myosin filaments, and extending from one Z band to the next.

Sarcopenia: A decline in muscle mass and strength with age.

Satellite cell: Unspecialized cells in muscle that can develop into muscle cells to repair muscle injuries.

Skeletal muscle: Striated muscle that produces voluntary movement.

Slow twitch: A type of muscle fiber that has slow contractile characteristics and a high capacity to use oxygen. Slow-twitch muscle fibers are also called Type I fibers.

Smooth muscle: Unstriated, involuntary muscle of the digestive and respiratory systems and some other organs.

Sphincter muscle: A circular muscle around a central opening that causes it to open and close, such as the muscle that prevents urine from leaking from the bladder.

Sprain: An injury to a ligament.

Stabilizer: A muscle that contracts without movement and holds a joint in position.

Strain: An injury to a muscle or tendon.

Strength: The ability of a muscle to exert force.

Stretch: The lengthening of a muscle produced without a nerve impulse.

Synergist: A muscle that assists another muscle to accomplish a movement.

Tendinitis: Inflammation of a tendon.

Tendon: A round cord or flat band that attaches skeletal muscle to bone.

Tendon transfer: Surgery in which doctors cut a tendon and reposition it so the muscle attached to it performs a different function.

Tetanus: A state of continuous muscular contraction. Tetanus is also called tetanic contraction.

Trichinellosis: Also trichinosis. A muscle disease caused by the parasite *Trichinella*.

Twitch: The response of a single muscle fiber to a single nerve impulse

Z line: The borderline region between two sarcomeres, where actin filaments come together.

SELECTED BIBLIOGRAPHY

Alexander, R. McNeill. *Exploring Biomechanics: Animals in Motion.* New York: Scientific American, 1992.

_____. *The Human Machine.* New York: Columbia University Press, 1992.

Bowden, Bradley, and Joan Bowden. *An Illustrated Atlas of the Skeletal Muscles.* Second Edition. Englewood, CO: Morton Publishing Company, 2005.

Delavier, Frédéric. *Strength Training Anatomy.* Second Edition. Champaign, IL: Human Kinetics, 2006.

Hawkes, Chris. *The Human Body.* Buffalo, NY: Firefly Books, 2006.

Jarmey, Chris. *The Concise Book of Muscles.* Berkeley, CA: Lotus Publishing, 2003.

Margulies, Sheldon. *The Fascinating Body: How It Works.* Lanham, MD: Scarecrow Education, 2004.

Metzl, Jordan, and Carol Shookhoff. *The Young Athlete: A Sports Doctor's Complete Guide for Parents.* Boston: Little Brown, 2002.

Monroe, Judy. *Steroids, Sports, and Body Image: The Risks of Performance-Enhancing Drugs.* Berkeley Heights, NJ: Enslow, 2004.

Navarra, Tova. *Your Body: Highlights of Human Anatomy.* Neptune, NJ: Asbury Park Press, 1990.

Pope, Harrison, Katharine Phillips, and Roberto Olivardia. *The Adonis Complex: The Secret Crises of Male Body Obsession.* New York: Free Press, 2000.

Siegel, Irwin M. *All About Muscle: A User's Guide.* New York: Demos Medical Publishing, 2000.

FOR FURTHER INFORMATION

Books

Alexander, R. McNeill. *Exploring Biomechanics: Animals in Motion*. New York: Scientific American, 1992.

_____. *The Human Machine*. New York: Columbia University Press, 1992.

Bowden, Bradley, and Joan Bowden. *An Illustrated Atlas of the Skeletal Muscles*. Second Edition. Englewood, CO: Morton Publishing Company, 2005.

Delavier, Frédéric. *Strength Training Anatomy*. Second Edition. Champaign, IL: Human Kinetics, 2006.

Hawkes, Chris. *The Human Body*. Buffalo, NY: Firefly Books, 2006.

Jarmey, Chris. *The Concise Book of Muscles*. Berkeley, CA: Lotus Publishing, 2003.

Margulies, Sheldon. *The Fascinating Body: How It Works*. Lanham, MD: Scarecrow Education, 2004.

Metzl, Jordan, and Carol Shookhoff. *The Young Athlete: A Sports Doctor's Complete Guide for Parents*. Boston: Little Brown, 2002.

Monroe, Judy. *Steroids, Sports, and Body Image: The Risks of Performance-Enhancing Drugs*. Berkeley Heights, NJ: Enslow, 2004.

Navarra, Tova. *Your Body: Highlights of Human Anatomy*. Neptune, NJ: Asbury Park Press, 1990.

Pope, Harrison, Katharine Phillips, and Roberto Olivardia. *The Adonis Complex: The Secret Crises of Male Body Obsession*. New York: Free Press, 2000.

Siegel, Irwin M. *All About Muscle: A User's Guide*. New York: Demos Medical Publishing, 2000.

Websites

http://health.howstuffworks.com/muscle.htm. This site features a wide range of information on the muscular system.

http://health.howstuffworks.com/framed.htm?parent=muscle.htm&url=http://www.sci.sdsu.edu/movies/actin_myosin_gif.html. Visit this site to see San Diego State University's 3-D animation of actin-myosin crossbridges.

http://www.nismat.org/physcor/muscle.html. This page from the Nicholas Institute of Sports Medicine and Athletic Trauma offers a good explanation of how muscles work.

http://www.edb.utexas.edu/ssn/IOC-%20Athlete_s%20Nutrit.pdf. Visit this link to download the International Olympic Committee's *Nutrition for Athletes* guidebook.

http://www.nsbri.org/HumanPhysSpace/. Learn about human physiology in space at the National Space Biomedical Research Institute site.

http://eap.jpl.nasa.gov. Visit NASA's webhub for electroactive polymer actuators. It includes links to artificial muscle laboratories and projects worldwide.

Agencies and Organizations

American Academy of Orthopaedic Surgeons
6300 North River Road
Rosemont, IL 60018
www.aaos.org
This organization provides information on the musculoskeletal system for orthopaedic patients and professionals.

American College of Sports Medicine
P.O. Box 1440
Indianapolis, IN 46206
www.acsm.org
This group publishes a quarterly newsletter entitled *Fit Society Page*.

Facioscapulohumeral Muscular Dystrophy Society
3 Westwood Road
Lexington, MA 02420
www.fshsociety.org
The society supports research and assists families affected by MD.

Genetic Alliance
4301 Connecticut Avenue, North West
Suite 404
Washington, DC 20008
www.geneticalliance.org
Search for information on any genetic disease in this organization's online database.

March of Dimes Birth Defects Foundation
1275 Mamaroneck Avenue
White Plains, NY 10605
www.marchofdimes.com
Publishes a free, monthly e-mail newsletter on birth defects of all kinds.

Muscular Dystrophy Association - USA
National Headquarters
3300 East Sunrise Drive
Tucson, AZ 85718
www.mda.org
Publishes a bimonthly magazine, *Quest*.

Muscular Dystrophy Family Foundation
Suite 100
3951 North Meridian Street
Indianapolis, IN 46208
www.mdff.org
This group provides support for individuals and families affected by neuromuscular diseases.

Myasthenia Gravis Foundation of America, Inc.
1821 University Avenue West
Suite S256
St. Paul, MN 55104
www.myasthenia.org
This volunteer association publishes the quarterly newsletter *Foundation Focus*.

The Myositis Association
1233 20th Street North West
Suite 402
Washington, DC 20036
www.myositis.org
Publishes a quarterly newsletter, *The Outlook*.

National Academy of Sports Medicine
26632 Agoura Road
Calabasas, CA 91302
www.nasm.org
Publishes a monthly newsletter, *Form*.

National Athletic Trainers' Association
2952 Stemmons Freeway #200
Dallas, TX 75247
www.nata.org
This group promotes athletic training as a career.

National Institute of Arthritis and Musculoskeletal and Skin Diseases
Information Clearinghouse
National Institutes of Health
1 AMS Circle
Bethesda, MD 20892
www.niams.nih.gov
Visit the website for factsheets on myopathies.

National Organization for Rare Disorders
55 Kenosia Avenue
P.O. Box 1968
Danbury, CT 06813
www.rarediseases.org
Maintains an online database of over 1,150 rare diseases.

National Space Biomedical Research Institute
One Baylor Plaza
NA-425
Houston, TX 77030
www.nsbri.org
Publishes *NSBRI Explorer*, a quarterly newsletter.

National Strength and Conditioning Association
1885 Bob Johnson Drive
Colorado Springs, CO 80906
www.nsca-lift.org
Visit the website for a free subscription to the *NSCA Performance Training Journal*.

Parent Project Muscular Dystrophy
1012 North University Boulevard
Middletown, OH 45042
www.parentprojectmd.org
Serves parents of children with Duchenne and Becker Muscular Dystrophy.

NOTES

1 Translated in Troels Kardel, *Steno on Muscles: Introduction, Texts, Translations* (Philadelphia: The American Philosophical Society, 1994), p. 219.

2 Matthew Cobb, "Reading and Writing *The Book of Nature*: Jan Swammerdam (1637–1680)," *Endeavour* (September 1, 2000), pp. 122–128.

3 Matthew Cobb, "Exorcising the Animal Spirits: Jan Swammerdam on Nerve Function," *Nature Reviews/Neuroscience* (May 2002), pp. 395–400.

4 Quoted in Cobb, 2002.

5 Kardel, p. 217.

6 Quoted in Cobb, 2002.

7 Irwin M. Siegel, *All About Muscle: A User's Guide.* (New York: Demos, 2000), p. xiii.

8 Estimates from Stephen P. Lahr, associate professor of physical therapy, Ithaca College, Ithaca, NY.

9 Siegel, p. 10.

10 Niels Moller and K. Sreekumaran Nair, "Regulation of Muscle Mass and Function: Effects of Aging and Hormones," in Board Institute of Medicine, *The Role of Protein and Amino Acids in Sustaining and Enhancing Performance* (Washington, DC: National Academy Press, 1999), p. 122.

11 Theodore Dimon, Jr., *Anatomy of the Moving Body: A Basic Course in Bones, Muscles, and Joints.* (Berkeley, CA: North Atlantic Books, 2001), p. 18.

12. T.J. Koob and Adam P. Summers, "Tendon—Bridging the Gap," *Comparitive Biochemistry and Physiology Part A* (December 2002), pp. 905–909.

13 Steven Vogel, *Prime Mover: A Natural History of Muscle* (New York: Norton, 2001), p. 121.

14 Douglas Syme, personal communication.

15 Vogel, p. 17.

16 Ibid.

17 T Pedersen, O. B. Nielsen, G. D. Lamb, and D. G. Stephenson, "Intracellular Acidosis Enhances the Excitability of Working Muscle," *Science* (August 20, 2004), pp. 1112–1113.

18 "The Athlete's Kitchen: What's New in Nutrition: Information from ACSM'a 2003 Annual Meeting," American College of Sports Medicine, *Fit Society Page*, (Summer 2003), p. 10.

19 Eric P. Widmaier, Hershel Raff, and Kevin T. Strang, *Vander's Human Physiology,* 10th Edition (Dubuque, IA: McGraw-Hill, 2006), pp. 284–285.

20 Vogel, p. 56–57.

21 Siegel, p. xviii.

22 Siegel, p. 41

23 Vogel, p. 23.

24 Siegel, p. xv.

25 Estimates of the number of cells in the human body range from 10 to 100 trillion. We used the highest from editors of Time-Life Books, *Mysteries of the Human Body* (Alexandria, VA: Time-Life, 1990), p. 19.

26 Siegel, p. xv.

27 Steve Giegerich, *Body of Knowledge: One Semester of Gross Anatomy, The Gateway to Becoming a Doctor* (New York: Scribner, 2001), p. 149.

28 Judy E. Anderson, "A Role for Nitric Oxide in Muscle Repair: Nitric Oxide-mediated Activation of Muscle Satellite Cells," *Molecular Biology of the Cell* (May 2000), pp. 1859–1874.

29 Rowan Hooper, "Mighty Mice Hold Key to Muscle-wasting Disease," *NewScientist* (December 10, 2005), p. 11.

30 R. McNeill Alexander, *Exploring Biomechanics* (New York; Scientific American Library, 1992), p.5.

31 Steven Vogel, personal communication.

32 Steven Vogel, personal communication.

33 Alexander, *Exploring Biomechanics*, p. 106.

34 J. Gros, M. Manceau, V. Thomé, and C. Marcelle, "A Common Somitic Origin for Embryonic Muscle Progentoris and Satellite Cells," *Nature* (June 16, 2005), pp. 954–958.

35 S. Iezzi, G. Cossu, C. Nervi, et al., "Stage-specific Modulation of Skeletal Myogenesis by Inhibitors of Nuclear Deacetylases," Proceedings of the National Academy of Sciences (May 28, 2002), pp. 7757–7762.

36 Weichun Lin, Robert W. Burgess, Bertha Dominguez, et al., "Distinct Roles of Nerve and Muscle in Postsynaptic Differentiation of the Neuromuscular Synapse," *Nature* (April 26, 2001), pp. 1057–1064.

37 Guoping Feng, Michael B. Laskowski, David A. Feldheim, et al., "Roles for Ephrins in Positionally Selective Synaptogenesis between Motor Neurons and Muscle Fibers," *Neuron* (February 2000), pp. 295–306.

38 Weichun Lin, Bertha Dominguez, Jiefei Yang, et al., "Neurotransmitter Acetylcholine Negatively Regulates Neuromuscular Synapse Formation by a Cdk5-Dependent Mechanism," *Neuron* (May 19, 2005), pp. 569–579.

39 Lewis Wolpert, *The Triumph of the Embryo* (Oxford: Oxford University Press, 1991), p. 147.

40 N. F. Butte, "Basal Metabolism of Infants," In Beat Schürch & Nevin S. Scrimshaw, (eds), International Dietary Energy Consultancy Group, *Activity, Energy Expenditure and Energy Requirements of Infants and Children*, (Proceedings of an I/D/E/C/G Workshop held in Cambridge, MA, USA, November 14 to 17, 1989).

41 Douglas A. Syme and Robert K. Josephson, "How to Build Fast Muscles: Synchronous and Asynchronous Designs," *Integrative and Comparative Biology* (August 2002), pp. 762–770.

42 Jan Adkins, *Moving Heavy Things*. (Brooklin, ME: AoodenBoat Publications, 2004), p. 4.

43 Stephen L. Katz, Douglas A. Syme, and Robert E. Shadwick, "High-speed Swimming: Enhanced Power in Yellowfin Tuna," *Nature* (April 12, 2001), pp. 770–771.

44 Ibid.

45 Douglas Syme, personal communication.

46 D. Young and H. Bennet-Clark, "The Role of the Tymbal in Cicada Sound Production," *Journal of Experimental Biology* (April 1995), pp. 1001–1020.

47 Syme and Josephson, 2002.

48 Douglas Syme, personal communication.

49 *The Columbia World of Quotations*. New York: Columbia University Press, 1996.

50 R. McNeill Alexander, *The Human Machine* (New York: Columbia University Press, 1992), p. 134.

51 H. Takemoto, "Morphological Analyses of the Human Tongue Musculature for Three-Dimensional Modeling," *Journal of Speech, Language, and Hearing Research* (February 2001), pp. 95–107.

52 Estimate from the *Mayo Clinic Health Letter* (February 2004), page numbers not available.

53 Bradley Bowden and Joan Bowden, *An Illustrated Atlas of the Skeletal Muscles* (Englewood, CO: Morton Publishing, 2001), p. 123.

54 Ira Sanders, "The Human Tongue Slows Down to Speak," presented at the annual meeting of the American Bronchoesophagological Association, May 2, 2003.

55 Dimon, page 89.

56 Siegel, p. 79.

57 Alexander, p. 20–21.

58 The Royal College of Surgeons of England, *Facial Transplantation, Working Party Report*, (November 2003), p. 10.

59 Mary Duenwald, "The Psychology of . . . Facial Expressions: Is She Hiding Something?" *Discover* (January 2005), pp. 16–17.

60 Roger Highfield, "Do You Fancy a New Face? Surgeons Could Transplant One Today," *The Telegraph* (London), October 22, 2003.

61 Editors of Time-Life Books, p. 64.

62 Tova Navarra, *Your Body: Highlights of Human Anatomy*, (Neptune, NJ: Asbury Park Press, 1990), p. 16.

63 Gary G. Matthews, *Cellular Physiology of Nerve & Muscle* (Palo Alto: Blackwell, 1986), p. 134.

64 R. P. Nolan, M. V. Kamath, J. S. Flora, et al., "Heart Rate Variability Biofeedback as a Behavioral Neurocardiac Intervention to Enhance Vagal Heart Rate Control," *American Heart Journal* (June 2005), p. 1137.

65 R. P. Nolan, personal communication.

66 Quote in Gina Kim, "Working with a Young Lance Armstrong," *Sacramento Bee* (July 14, 2005), available online at http://www.usoc.org/11796_35583.htm.

67 Suzanne Halliburton, "Tour de France: Lance in Seventh Heaven," *Grand Forks Herald*, available at www.grandforks.com.

68 A. Lucia, J. Hoyos, and J. L. Chicharro, "Physiology of Professional Road Cycling," *Sports Medicine* (volume 31, number 5, month not available, 2001), pp. 325–337.

69 Lance Armstrong with Sally Jenkins, *It's Not About the Bike: My Journey Back to Life*, (New York: Berkeley Books, 2001), p. 3.

70 Lucia et al.

71 Edward F. Coyle, "Improved Muscular Efficiency Displayed as Tour de France Champion Matures," *Journal of Applied Physiology* (June 2005), pp. 2191–2196.

72 Armstrong and Jenkins, p. 4.

73 Quoted in "Looking at Lance Through a Physiological Lens," press release from The American Physiological Society, June 14, 2005.

74 Coyle.

75 Coyle, p. 2194.

76 E. F. Coyle, M. E. Feltner, S. A. Kautz, et al., "Physiological and Biomechanical Factors Associated with Elite Endurance Cycling Performance," *Medicine & Science in Sports & Exercise* (January 1991), pp. 93–107.

77 Armstrong and Jenkins, p. 63.

78 Quoted in Halliburton.

79 Quote Garden at http://www.quotegarden.com/exercise.html.

80 Y. W. Chen, M. J. Hubal, E. P. Hoffman, et al., "Molecular Responses of Human Muscle to Eccentric Exercise," *Journal of Applied Physiology* (December 2003), pp. 2485–2494

81 Vogel, p. 90.

82 Siegel, p. 21.

83 Jordan Metzl and Carol Shookhoff, *The Young Athlete: A Sports Doctor's Complete Guide for Parents* (Boston: Little Brown, 2002), p. 162

84 P. M. Clarkson and M. J. Hubal, "Exercise-induced Muscle Damage in Humans," *American Journal of Physical Medicine and Rehabilitation* (November 2002), S52–S69.

85 Ibid.

86 J. Z. Liu, R. W. Brown, and G. H. Yue, "A Dynamic Model of Muscle Activation, Fatigue, and Recovery," *Biophysical Journal* (May 2002), pp. 2344–2359.

87 A. St Clair Gibson and T. D. Noakes, "Evidence for Complex System Integration and Dynamic Neural Regulation of Skeletal Muscle Recruitment during Exercise in Humans," *British Journal of Sports Medicine* (December 2004), pp. 797–806.

88 A. St Clair Gibson, E. J. Schabort, and T. D. Noakes, "Reduced Neuromuscular Activity and Force Generation during Prolonged Cycling," *American Journal of Physiology – Regulatory, Integrative and Comparative Physiology* (July 2001), pp. R187–R196.

89 Rick Lovett, "Running on Empty," *NewScientist* (March 20, 2004), p. 43.

90 Ibid, p. 44.

91 F. H. Lindsay, J. A. Hawley, K. H. Myburgh, et al., "Improved Athletic Performance in Highly Trained Cyclists after Interval Training," *Medicine & Science in Sports & Exercise* (November 1996), pp. 1427–1434.

92 S. B. Thacker, J. Gilchrist, D. Stroup, et. al., "The Impact of Stretching on Sports Injury Risk: A Systematic Review of the Literature," *Medicine & Science in Sports & Exercise*, (March 2004), pp. 371–378.

93 Metzl and Shookhoff, p. 113.

94 "Flexibility in Aging: Stretching to Mend the Bend," American College of Sports Medicine, *ACSM Fit Society Page*, (Summer 2003), p. 5.

95 Metzl and Shookhoff, p. 163.

96 M. Burgemesiter, "Exercise Right: Proper Warm-up and Cool Down," American College of Sports Medicine, *ACSM Fit Society Page*, (Spring 2005), pp. 3–4. Excerpted with permission.

97 Quoted in Mary Strote, "How Strong Muscles Build Strong Bones," *Shape* (May 2003), page numbers not available. For details of the study, see Jasminka Ilich-Ernst, Rhonda A. Brownbill, , Martha A. Ludemann, and Rongwei Fu, "Critical Factors for Bone Health in Women Across the Age Span: How Important Is Muscle Mass?" at http://www.medscape.com/viewarticle/432910

98 William J. Evans, "Protein Nutrition, Exercise and Aging," *Journal of the American College of Nutrition*, (December 2004, supplement), pp. 601S–609S.

99 Ibid.

100 Anne Marie W. Petersen and Bente Klarlund Pedersen, "The Anti-inflammatory Effect of Exercise," *Journal of Applied Physiology* (April 2005), pp. 1154–1162.

101 Quoted in "Many Body-Conscious Teens Use Supplements to Improve Physique," press release from Children's' Hospital Boston, July 27, 2005.

102 Ibid.

103 Alison E. Field, S. Bryn Austin, Carlos A. Camargo, Jr., et al., "Exposure to the Mass Media, Body Shape Concerns, and Use of Supplements to Improve Weight and Shape Among Male and Female Adolescents," *Pediatrics* (August 2005), pp. e214–e220.

104 Bryan W. Smith, "Q&A with ACSM," *ACSM Fit Society Page* (Summer 2002), p. 2.

105 Op cit.

106 P. Obert, S. Mandigout, A Vinet, et al., "Effect of Aerobic Training and Detraining on Left Ventricular Dimensions and Diastolic Function in Prepubertal Boys and Girls," *International Journal of Sports Medicine* (February 2001), pp. 90–96.

107 "Types of Exercise" from *The Washington Post* online at www.washingtonpost.com

108 Boaz D. Rosen, Thor Edvardsen, Shenghan Lai, et al., "Left Ventricular Concentric Remodeling Is Associated With Decreased Global and Regional Systolic Function: The Multi-Ethnic Study of Atherosclerosis," Circulation (August 16, 2005), pp. 984–991.

109 Edward H. Nessel, "Even My Eyebrows Hurt!" available online at www.swimmingcoach.org.

110 Ibid.

111 D.A. Jones, D. J. Newham, and P.M. Clarkson, "Skeletal Muscle Stiffness and Pain Following Eccentric Exercise of the Elbow Flexors," *Pain* (August 1987), pp. 233–242.

112 T. S. Talag, "Residual Muscular Soreness as Influenced by Concentric, Eccentric, and Static Contractions," *Research Quarterly* (December 1973), pp. 458–469.

113 Ibid.

114 Ibid.

115 J. Maes and L. Kravitz, "Treating and Preventing DOMS," *IDEA Personal Trainer* (July–August 2003), p. 41.

116 J. S. Kim, K. W. Hinchcliff, M. Yamaguchi, et al., "Exercise Training Increases Oxidative Capacity and Attenuates Exercise-induced Ultrastructural Damage in Skeletal Muscle of Aged Horses," *Journal of Applied Physiology* (January 2005), pp. 334–342.

117 "Exercising When It Hurts," *Mayo Clinic Women's HealthSource* (September 2004), p. 7.

118 Jim Thome quoted at http://www.brainyquote.com/quotes/quotes/j/jimthome211395.html.

119 Sheldon Margulies, *The Fascinating Body: How It Works* (Lanham, MD: Scarecrow Education, 2004), pp. 186–187.

120 J. M. Grimes, L. A. Ricci, and R. H. Melloni, Jr. "Plasticity in Anterior Hypothalamic Vasopressin Correlates with Aggression during Anabolic-Androgenic Steroid Withdrawal in Hamsters," *Behavioral Neuroscience* (February 2006), 115–124.

121 Dr. Melloni is quoted in "Anabolic Steroids Flip the Adolescent's Brain Switch for Aggressive Behavior," press release from the American Psychological Association, February 21, 2006.

122 Dr. Plancher is quoted in "Clarifying Steroid-related Confusion: Sports Orthopaedics Expert Kevin Plancher, M.D., on Positive Uses for Steroids in Medicine," press release from MCPR Public Relations, Greenwich, CT, June 2005.

123 K. Johns, M. J. Beddall, and R. C. Corrin. "Anabolic Steroids for the Treatment of Weight Loss in HIV-infected Individuals," *Cochrane Database of Systematic Reviews* October 2005), 194, p. CD005483.

124 Plancher, op cit.

125 Ibid.

126 Ibid.

127 Ibid.

128 Adapted from President's Council on Physical Fitness and Sports, "Anabolic-Androgenic Steroids: Incidence of Use and Health Implications," *Research Digest* (March 2005), p. 5. Original source cited as M. S. Bahrke and C. E. Yesalius, *Performance-Enhancing Substances in Sports and Exercise* (Champaign, IL: Human Kinetics, 2002).

129 Susan Sontag, *Illness as Metaphor* (New York: Vintage Books, 1977), 1.

130 P. Hansen, P. Aagaard, M. Kjaer, et al., "Effect of Habitual Running on Human Achilles Tendon Load-deformation Properties and Cross-sectional Area," *Journal of Applied Physiology* (December 2003), p. 2376.

131 Quote in "Overuse Injuries Most Common Injury Associated with Running," press release from the American Academy of Orthopaedic Surgeons, March 4, 2003.

132 Randi Hutter Epstein, "For Muscle Injuries, Many Treatments but Little Evidence," *New York Times*, February 2, 2002.

133 Reprinted from "Activity Health Tip #3: R.I.C.E." with permission from the National Athletic Trainers' Association and author Mary Kirkland, ATC/L.

134 Bowden and Bowden, p. 128.

135 Data from the American Association of Neurological Surgeons.

136 Jessica Smith, "Safety Principles of BODYPUMP," *American Fitness* (July 2001), page numbers not available.

137 William S. Marras, Kermit G. Davis, Sue A. Ferguson, et al. "Spine Loading Characteristics of Patients with Low Back Pain Compared with Asymptomatic Individuals," *Spine* (December 1, 2001), pp. 2566–2574.

138 Quoted in John O'Neil, "Vital Signs: Prevention; New Advice to Avoid More Back Pain," *The New York Times*, December 4, 2001.

139 Quoted in "Moving this October? Here's How to Reduce Your Back Injury Risk," press release from the American Academy of Orthopaedic Surgeons, September 26, 2001.

140 G. Hilde, K.B. Hagen, G. Jamtvedt, and M. Winnem, "Advice to Stay Active as a Single Treatment for Low-back Pain and Sciatica," *The Cochrane Database of Systematic Reviews* (2001, Issue 4, Article number CD003632).

141 M. van Tulder, A. Malmivaara, R Esmail, and B. Koes, "Exercise Therapy for Low Back Pain: A Systematic Review within the Framework of the Cochrane Collaboration Back Review Group," *Spine* (November 1, 2000), pp. 2784–2796.

142 Siegfried Mense and David G. Simons, *Muscle Pain: Understanding Its Nature, Diagnosis, and Treatment* (Philadelphia: Lippincott Williams & Wilkins, 2001), p. 113.

143 J. M. Purvis and R. G. Burke, "Recreational Injuries in Children: Incidence and Prevention," *Journal of the American Academy of Orthopaedic Surgeons* (November/December 2001), pp. 365–374.

144 All statistics for this answer and for the accompanying graphs from John W. Powell and Kim D. Barber-Foss, "Injury Patterns in Selected High School Sports: A Review of the 1995–1997 Seasons," *Journal of Athletic Training* (September 1999), pp. 277–284.

145 W. D. McArdle, F. I Katch, and V. L. Katch, *Exercise Physiology: Energy, Nutrition, and Human Performance*, Fifth Edition, (Philadelphia: Lippincott Williams & Wilkins, 2001), p. 489.

146 McArdle et al., p. 491

147 R. Olivardia, H. G. Pope, Jr., and J. I. Hudson, "Muscle Dysmorphia in Male Weightlifters: A Case-Control Study," *American Journal of Psychiatry* (August 2000), pp. 1291–1296.

148 Mike Cardwell, "Muscle Dysmorphia," *Psychology Review* (April 2001), p. 34.

149 G. Cafri, J. K. Thompson, L. Ricciardelli, et al., "Pursuit of the Muscular Ideal: Physical and Psychological Consequences and Putative Risk Factors," *Clinical Psychology Review* (February 2005), pp. 215–239.

150 H. G. Pope, Jr., A. J. Gruber, B. Mangweth, et al., "Body Image Perception among Men in Three Countries" *American Journal of Psychiatry* (August 2000), pp. 1297–1301.

151 Siegel, p. 91.

152 Hansen et al., pp. 2375–2380.

153 Steven A. Moore, Fumiaki Saito, Jianguo Chen, et al., "Deletion of Brain Dystroglycan Recapitulates Aspects of Congenital Muscular Dystrophy," *Nature* (July 25, 2002), pp. 422–425.

154 Estimate from the Centers for Disease Control and Prevention.

155 Estimates from the FacioScapuloHumeral Muscular Dystrophy Society.

156 Estimate from the Cleveland Clinic.

157 Quoted in "Enzyme Halts Muscle Waste in Mouse Model," press release from the University of California, San Diego, April 17, 2002.

158 Ami Mankodi, Masanori P. Takahashi, Hong Jiang, et al. "Expanded CUG Repeats Trigger Aberrant Splicing of ClC-1 Chloride Channel Pre-mRNA and Hyperexcitability of Skeletal Muscle in Myotonic Dystrophy," *Molecular Cell* (July 2002), pp. 35–44.

159 D. Bansal, K. Miyake, S. Vogel, et al. "Defective Membrane Repair in Dysferlin-deficient Muscular Dystrophy," *Nature* (May 8, 2003), pp. 168–172.

160 Estimate from the Mayo Clinic.

161 R. T. Moxley, III, S. Ashwal, S. Pandya, et al., "Practice Parameter: Corticosteroid Treatment of Duchenne Dystrophy: Report of the Quality Standards Subcommittee of the American Academy of Neurology and the Practice Committee of the Child Neurology Society," *Neurology* (January 11, 2005), pp. 13–20.

162 Yongping Yue, Zhenbo Li, Scott Q. Harper, et al. "Microdystrophin Gene Therapy of Cardiomyopathy Restores Dystrophin-Glycoprotein Complex and Improves Sarcolemma Integrity in the Mdx Mouse Heart," *Circulation* (September 30, 2003), pp. 1626–1632.

163 Paul Gregorevic, Michael J Blankinship, James M Allen, et al. "Systemic Delivery of Genes to Striated Muscles Using Adeno-associated Viral Vectors," *Nature Medicine* (August 2004), pp. 828–834.

164 Quoted in "Virus Delivers Dystrophin to Mice with Muscular Dystrophy," press release from the University of Michigan, October 29, 1997.

165 Estimate from the National Institute of Neurological Disorders and Stroke.

166 L. H. Phillips, II, "The Epidemiology of Myasthenia Gravis," *Annals of the New York Academy of Sciences* (September 2003), pp. 407–412.

167 M. A. Agius, D. P. Richman, R. H. Fairclough, et al., "Three Forms of Immune Myasthenia," *Annals of the New York Academy of Sciences* (September 2003), pp. 453–456.

168 According to the Muscular Dystrophy Association.

169 D. P. Richman and M. A. Agius, "Treatment Principles in the Management of Autoimmune Myasthenia Gravis," *Annals of the New York Academy of Sciences* (September 2003), pp. 457–472.

170 G. E. Yousef, D.A. Isenberg, and J. F. Mowbray, "Detection of Enterovirus Specific RNA Sequences in Muscle Biopsy Specimens from Patients with Adult Onset Myositis," *Annals of the Rheumatic Diseases* (May 1990), pp. 310–315.

171 S. L. Roy, A. S. Lopez, and P. M. Schantz, "Trichinellosis Surveillance—United States, 1997–2001," CDC: Morbidity and Mortality Weekly Report (July 25, 2003), pp. 1–8.

172 All quotations from Shari Works are personal communications.

173 Quoted in Janet Carey Eldred, *Sentimental Attachments: Essays, Creative Nonfiction, and Other Experiments in Composition* (Portsmouth, NH: Heinemann, 2005), p. 69.

174 Chris Jarmey, *The Concise Book of Muscles* (Berkeley, CA: North Atlantic Books, 2003), p. 63.

175 W. D. McArdle, F. I. Katch, and V. L. Katch, *Exercise Physiology: Energy, Nutrition, and Human Performance*, Fifth Edition, (Philadelphia: Lippincott Williams & Wilkins, 2001), p. 306.

176 McArdle et al., p. 320.

177 Geoffrey P. Dobson, personal communication.

178 M. Hernandez, "La Movilidad del Pabellon Auditivo," *Trab. Antropol.* (1980), pp. 199–203

179 Davidson, personal communication.

180 Blue Histology - Male Reproductive System, School of Anatomy and Human Biology, University of Western Australia, available online at http://www.lab.anhb.uwa.edu.au

181 Garry Wilkes, "Hiccups," May 24, 2005, at http://www.emedicine.com/emerg/topic252.htm (May 30, 2007).

182 S. Osman Hussain, John C. Barbato, Lauren G. Koch, et al., "Cardiac Function in Rats Selectively Bred for Low- and High-capacity Running," *American Journal of Physiology – Regulatory, Integrative and Comparative Physiology* (December 2001), pp. R1787–R1791.

183 Douglas Syme, personal communication.

184 A. Danis, Y. Kyriazis, and V. Klissouras, "The Effect of Training in Male Prepubertal and Pubertal Monozygotic Twins." *European Journal of Applied Physiology* (May 2003), pp. 309–318.

185 R. S. Mazzeo, P. Cavanaugh, W. J. Evans, et al., "Exercise and Physical Activity for Older Adults," *Medicine and Science in Sports and Exercise* (June 1998). A position statement of the American College of Sports Medicine.

186 Ibid.

187 Michael G. Bemben, "The Physiology of Aging: What You Can Do to Slow or Stop the Loss of Muscle Mass," *American Fitness* (May-June 2002), p. 262.

188 Mazzeo et al.

189 M. J. Toth, D. E. Matthews, R. P. Tracy, and M. J. Previs, "Age-related Differences in Skeletal Muscle Protein Synthesis: Relation to Markers of Immune Activation," *American Journal of Physiology - Endocrinology and Metabolism* (May 2005), pp. E883–E891.

190 Kevin R. Short, Maureen L. Bigelow, Jane Kahl, et. al., "Decline in Skeletal Muscle Mitochondrial Function with Aging in Humans," *Proceedings of the National Academy of Sciences* (April 12, 2005), pp. 5618–5623

191 D. Paddon-Jones, M. Sheffield-Moore, X-J Zhang, et al., "Amino Acid Ingestion Improves Protein Synthesis in the Young and the Elderly," *American Journal of Physiology - Endocrinology and Metabolism* (March 2004), pp. E321–E328.

192 K. R. Short, J. L, Vittone, M. L. Bigelow, et al., "Age and Aerobic Exercise Training Effects on Whole Body and Muscle Protein Metabolism," *American Journal of Physiology - Endocrinology and Metabolism* (January 2004), pp. E92–E101.

193 Janet Raloff, "Vanishing Flesh: Muscle Loss in the Elderly Finally Gets Some Respect," *Science News* (August 10, 1996), p. 90.

194 S. Goldin-Meadow, H. Nusbaum, S. Kelly, and S. Wagner, "Explaining Math: Gesturing Lightens the Load," *Psychological Science* (November 2001), pp. 516–522.

195 Spencer D. Kelly and Leslie H. Goldsmith, "Gesture and Right Hemisphere Involvement in Evaluating Lecture Material," *Gesture* (January 2004), pp. 25–42.

196 T. Tamura, S. Miyasako, M. Ogawa, et al., "Assessment of Bed Temperature Monitoring for Detecting Body Movement During Sleep: Comparison with Simultaneous Video Image Recording and Actigraphy," *Medical Engineering & Physics* (February 1999), pp. 1–8.

197 "In the Dead of the Night," *The Observer* (U.K.), November 18, 2001.

198 Jing Z. Liu, Zu Y. Shan, Lu D. Zhang, et al., "Human Brain Activation during Sustained and Intermittent Submaximal Fatigue Muscle Contractions: An fMRI Study," *Journal of Neurophysiology* (July 2003), pp. 300–312.

199 Quoted in Betty Weider, "Down But Not Out: Lessons from the Pros for Recovery and Rehab after Injury," *Muscle & Fitness* (June 2003), p. 62.

200 D. P. Ferris, K. E. Gordon, J. A. Beres-Jones, and S. J. Harkema, "Muscle Activation during Unilateral Stepping Occurs in the Nonstepping Limb of Humans with Clinically Complete Spinal Cord Injury," *Spinal Cord* (January 2004), pp. 14–23.

201 V. K. Ranganathan, V. Siemionow, J. Z. Liu, et al., "From Mental Power to Muscle Power— Gaining Strength by Using the Mind," *Neuropsychologia* (Volume 42, issue 7, 2004), pp. 944–956.

202 Lincoln E. Ford, *Muscle Physiology and Cardiac Function* (Traverse City, MI: Cooper, 2000).

203 Lincoln E. Ford, A. J. Detterline, L. K. Ho, and W. Cao, "Gender- and Height-related limits of Muscle Strength in World Weightlifting Champions," *Journal of Applied Physiology* (September 2000), pp. 1061–1064.

204 I. G. Brodsky, P. Balagopal, and K.S. Nair, "Effects of Testosterone Replacement on Muscle Mass and Muscle Protein Synthesis in Hypogonadal Men," *Journal of Clinical Endocrinology and Metabolism* (October 1996), pp. 3469–3475.

205 Estimate from the American Physiological Society.

206 Sandra K. Hunter, Ashley Critchlow, In-Sik Shin, and Roger M. Enoka, "Men Are More Fatiguable than Strength-matched Women When Performing Intermittent Submaximal Contractions," *Journal of Applied Physiology* (June 2004), pp. 2125–2132.

207 M. J. Hubal, H. Gordish-Dressman, P. D. Thompson, et al., "Variability in Muscle Size and Strength Gain after Unilateral Resistance Training," *Medicine & Science in Sports & Exercise* (June 2005), pp. 964–972.

208 Clarkson and Hubal, S52–S69.

209 D.E. Treaster and D. Burr, " Gender Differences in Prevalence of Upper Extremity Musculoskeletal Disorders," *Ergonomics* (April 15, 2004), pp. 495–526.

210 Timothy R. Jones, Peter A Humphrey, and Daniel C. Brennan. "Transplantation of Vascularized Allogeneic Skeletal Muscle for Scalp Reconstruction in a Renal Transplant Patient," *Transplantation* (June 27, 1998), pp. 1605–1610.

211 F. D. Pagani, H. DerSimonian, A. Zawadzka, et al., "Autologous Skeletal Myoblasts Transplanted to Ischemia-Damaged Myocardium in Humans," *Journal of the American College of Cardiology* (March 5, 2003), pp. 879–888

212 Quoted in "Team Reports First Direct Evidence That Transplanted Muscle Cells Can Take Root in Damaged Hearts," press release from the University of Michigan Health System, November 18, 2002.

213 Yen-Chih Huang, Robert G. Dennis, Lisa Larking, and Keither Baar, "Rapid Formation of Functional Muscles in Vitro Using Fibrin Gels," *Journal of Applied Physiology*, (February 2005), pp. 706–713.

214 Shulamit Levenberg, Jeroen Rouwkema, Mara Macdonald, et al., "Engineering Vascularized Skeletal Muscle Tissue," *Nature Biotechnology* (July 2005), pp. 879–884.

215 Quoted in "Scientists Create Replacement Muscle with Built-In Blood Supply," press release from the American Technion Society, June 17, 2005.

216 John M. Leferovich, Khamilia Bedelbaeva, Stefan Samulewicz, et al., "Heart Regeneration in Adult MRL Mice," *Proceedings of the National Academy of Sciences* (August 14, 2001), pp. 9830–9835.

217 Nicholas Wade, "The Uncertain Science of Growing Heart Cells," *The New York Times*, March 14, 2005.

218 Cynthia Fox, "Can Stem Cells Save Dying Hearts?" *Discover* (September 2005), pp. 58–61.

219 L. C. Amado, A. P. Saliaris, K. H. Schuleri, et al., "Cardiac Repair with Intramyocardial Injection of Allogenic Mesenchymal Stem Cells after Myocardial Infarction," *Proceedings of the National Academy of Sciences* (August 9, 2005), pp. 11474–11479

220 Bar-Cohen quoted in the Discovery Channel's *Daily Planet*, March 15, 2005.

221 Bar-Cohen quoted in Charli Schuler, "Scientists 'Muscle' Sci-Fi into Reality," *NASA News*, June 3, 2002.

222 M. Shahinpoor and K. J. Kim, "Ionic Polymer-metal Composites: III. Modeling and Simulation as Biomeimetic Sensors, Actuators, Transducers, and Artificial Muscles," *Smart Materials Structure* (volume 14, 2004), p. 1362

223 M. Shahinpoor and K. J. Kim, "Ionic Polymer-metal Composites: I. Fundamentals," *Smart Materials Structure* (volume 10, 2001), p. 819.

224 Dan Ferber, "Will Artificial Muscles Make You Stronger?" *Popular Science* (September 2003), page numbers not available.

225 Quoted in "Spontaneous Movement after Brain Death," press release from the American Academy of Neurology, January 11, 2000.

226 G. Saposnik, J. A. Bueri, R. Mauriño, R. Saizar, and N. S. Garretto, "Spontaneous and Reflex Movements in Brain Death," *Neurology* (January 2000), p. 221.

227 Op cit.

228 Douglas Syme, personal communication.

229 Ibid.

230 Ibid.

231 "Space Quotes" at http://www1.jsc.nasa.gov/er/seh/quotes.html.

232 McArdle et al., p. 712.

233 Caiozzo quoted in "Space Cycle Tests Artificial Gravity as Solution to Muscle Loss," press release from the National Space Biomedical Research Institute, September 14, 2005.

234 Robert H. Fitts, Danny R. Riley, and Jeffrey J. Widrick, "Physiology of a Microgravity Environment: Invited Review: Microgravity and Skeletal Muscle," *Journal of Applied Physiology* (August 2000), p. 823.

235 Ibid.

236 S. M. C. Lee, K. Cobb, J. Loehr, et al., "Foot-Ground Reaction Force During Resistive Exercise in Parabolic Flight," *Aviation, Space, and Environmental Medicine* (May 25, 2005), pp. 405–412.

237 Quoted in "Nutritional Supplements May Combat Muscle Loss," press release from the National Space Biomedical Research Institute, August 27, 2002.

238 S. Trappe, T. Trappe, P. Gallagher, et al., "Human Single Muscle Fibre Function with 84 Day Bedrest and Resistance Exercise," *The Journal of Physiology* (June 2004), pp. 501–513.

239 M. M. Bamman, G. R. Hunter, B. R. Stevens, et al., "Resistance Exercise Prevents Plantar Flexor Deconditioning During Bed Rest," *Medicine & Science in Sports & Exercise* (November 1997), pp. 1462–1468.

240 S. S. Schneider, W. E. Amonette, K. Blazine, et al., "Training with the International Space Station Interim Resistive Exercise Device," *Medicine & Science in Sports & Exercise*, (November 2003), pp. 1935–1945.

241 Quoted in Marc Ransford, "Resistance Training May Help Astronauts on Long Space Flights," NewsCenter (Ball State Campus Headlines) August 23, 2004, http://www.bsu.edu/news/article/0,1370,-1019-24016,00.html (May 30, 2007).

242 Carl Sagan quotes at http://www.thinkexist.com/english/Author/x/Author_2479_1.htm.

INDEX

abdominal muscles, 18, 54–55
abduction, 15
abductor pollicis brevis muscle, 58
acetylcholine, 30–31
acetylcholinesterase, 31
actin, 21, 22
adduction, 15
adductor pollicis muscle, 58
ADP (adenosine diphosphate), 25
aerobic metabolism, 26, 29
age and muscle mass, 127–128
aggression and steroids, 85–86
agonists and antagonists, 19
aldosterone, 85
American Academy of Orthopaedic Surgeons, 157
American College of Sports Medicine, 157
anaerobic metabolism, 25–26, 29
animals, muscles in, 40–43
aponeurosis, 18
arm muscles, 17, 58
Armstrong, Lance, 65–68
artificial muscles, 139–140
asthma, 32
asynchronous muscles, 43
ATP (adenosine triphosphate), 24–26, 29, 42, 70

atrophy, muscle, 145–146
auricularis muscles, 123–124
autoimmune diseases, 111

back muscles, 18, 53–54
back pain, 92–94
basal metabolism, 14
bike riding and muscle injury, 95–96
bipennate muscles, 17
black bears, 42
bladder muscle, 56
body weight, 32
bone health, 76
brain activity and muscle fatigue, 72–74
breathing process, muscles, 50–52
bundle of His, 62, 63
bursas, 18

cancer in muscles, 114–115
cardiac muscle
   and athletic capacity, 125–126
   contraction, 31
   defined, 12, 13
   and exercise, 81
   fatigue, 121–122
   process, 62–64
   stem cells to repair, 138–139
cardiac sphincter, 49, 50

cardiomyopathy, 81
cerebral palsy, 113
chewing, 47
children
   strength training, 70
   stretching, 74–75
cicadas, 42–43
ciliary muscles, 60
circulation, blood, 52
coccygeus muscle, 50
collagen, 20
concentric contraction, 27, 77
congenital myasthenia, 109
contraction, muscle
   force and length, 27
   process, 20–24
   twitch phases, 28
   twitch speeds of fibers, 29–30
   types, 26–27
corrugator muscle, 59
corticosteroids, 86
cortisol, 85
creatine, 80
cycling, 65–68

death and muscles, 141–142
defecation, 50
dehydration, 91
delayed onset muscle soreness (DOMS), 81–83

depression, 15
depressor anguli oris muscle, 59
depressor labii inferioris muscle, 59
diaphragm, 51–52
digestive system muscles, 49–50
disc herniation, 93
diseases
   cancer, 114–115
   infectious muscle diseases, 111–113
   muscular dystrophy, 105–108
   myasthenia, 109–111
   myopathies, 104–105
   rhabdomyolysis, 113–114
   See also injuries and diseases, muscle
DOMS treatment, 82
dorsiflexion, 16
Duchenne MD, 105, 107
dysmorphia, muscle, 99
dysphagia, 49

ear movement, 123–124
eating, muscles used in, 46–50
eccentric contraction, 27, 77, 82
electroactive polymers (EAPs), 139–140
elevation, 15
embryo development, 37–39
endurance training, 81
energy storage, 14
epiglottis, 48
erector pili, 14
exercise
   and bone strength, 76
   and cardiac muscle, 81
   cross-transfer, 130
   and immune system, 78–79
   and improved athletic capacity, 126
   interval training, 74
   mental imagery and, 130–131

and muscle damage, 71, 77
muscle fatigue, 71–74
muscle repair, 83
and muscle soreness, 81–83
and muscle strength, 69–71
and nutritional supplements, 79–80
strength training, 70, 77–78
stretching muscles, 74–75
warm-ups and cool downs, 75–76
while hurt, 83
extension, 15
external intercostal muscles, 51
external oblique muscle, 55
eyelids, 60
eye muscles, 30, 60–61

facial muscles, 17, 58–60
Facioscapulohumeral MD, 105
Facioscapulohumeral Muscular Dystrophy Society, 157
fast/slow muscles, 40–42
fat, 126–127
fatigue, muscle, 71–74
flexibility training, 74–75
flexion, 15
flexor pollicis brevis muscle, 58
force, muscle, 35, 41
fusiform muscles, 17

gas gangrene, 112
gastroesophageal reflux, 49
gastrulation, 37
gender issues, 133–134
gene therapy, for MD, 107–108
Genetic Alliance, 158
genioglossus muscle, 47
gluteus maximus muscle, 33, 35
glycholysis, 26
glycogen, 14, 26
gravity, 143–147

hamstring muscle, 19, 35, 57

hamstring tears, 89
hand muscles, 57–58
headaches, 94–95
heart muscle. See cardiac muscle
heart rate control, 64
heat, producing, 14
hemorrhoids, 50
hernias, 92
hiccups, 125
histamine, 32
hyoid bone, 47, 52
hyperextension, 15
hypertrophy, 77

iliocostalis thoracis muscle, 18
immune system and exercise, 78–79
infectious muscle diseases, 111–113
inferior rectus muscle, 60
injuries and diseases, muscle
   back pain, 92–94
   cancer, 114–115
   causes, 88–90
   DOMS treatment, 82
   headaches, 94–95
   hernias, 92
   infectious muscle diseases, 111–113
   muscle cramps, 91
   muscular dystrophy, 105–108
   myasthenia, 109–111
   myopathies, 104–105
   myositis, 111
   nutrition, 119
   posture, 119
   prevention, 102–103
   recreation and sports causes, 95–97
   R.E.S.T.S. prevention, 102–103
   rhabdomyolysis, 113–114
   R.I.C.E. treatment, 90–91
   sports overtraining, 98–100

sprains and strains, 90.
stitches, 92
tendinitis, 103
torn rotator cuffs, 100–102
inner thigh muscles, 57
interleukin-6 (IL-6), 78
internal oblique muscle, 55
iRED (interim Resistive Exercise
        Device), 146, 147
ischiocavernosus muscle, 124
isometric contraction, 26–27

jaw muscles, 46–47
joints, 18

kissing, 60

lactic acid, 26, 72
larynx, 52
lateral rectus muscle, 60
leg muscles, 17
    relationships, 19
    soleus, 30
leiomyoma, 114–115
leiomyosarcoma, 115
levator labii superioris alaeque
        nasi muscle, 59
levator labii superioris muscle,
        59
levator palpebrae superioris
        muscle, 33, 59
ligaments, 18
lips, 59
lower esophageal sphincter, 49,
        50
lungs, 51–52

mantis shrimp, 41
March of Dimes Birth Defects
        Foundation, 158
masseter muscle, 46
medial rectus muscle, 60
mesentery membranes, 54

metabolism
    aerobic, 26
    anaerobic, 25–26
mitochondria, 25, 70
motor nerves, 23, 38
motor neurons, 30–32, 38
multiple sclerosis, 113
muscle cells
    energy source, 24–26
    growth, 34
    mitochondria, 25
    transplanting, 135–136
muscle cramps, 91
muscle development, pre-birth,
        37–39
muscle fibers, 13
muscles
    and aging, 127–128
    and body weight, 32
    and bone health, 76
    contraction process, 20–24
    denseness versus fat,
        126–127
    efficiency, 36
    energy source, 24–26
    fatigue, 71–74
    force and power, 35–36
    functions of, 13–14
    growing, outside body, 137
    growth of, 34, 69–71
    movement after death, 141
    naming, 44–45
    number of, 32–33
    sizes of, 33, 35, 70
    in space, 143–147
    tone, 34
    transplanting, 135–136
    types of, 11–12
    volume, 8–9
muscular dystrophy, 35,
        105–108
Muscular Dystrophy
        Association - USA, 158

Muscular Dystrophy Family
        Foundation, 158
myasthenia gravis, 109–111
Myasthenia Gravis Foundation
        of America, Inc., 158
myoblast cells, 38, 137
myofibrils, 20–24
myokines, 78
myopathies, 104–105
myosin, 21, 22
myositis, 111
Myositits Association, 158
myostatin, 35
Myotonic MD, 106

naming muscles, 44–45
National Academy of Sports
        Medicine, 159
National Athletic Trainers'
        Association, 159
National Institute of Arthritis
        and Musculoskeletal and
        Skin Diseases, 159
National Organization for Rare
        Disorders, 159
National Space Biomedical
        Research Institute, 159
National Strength and
        Conditioning Association,
        159
neuromuscular junctions, 31, 38
neurotransmitters, 30–31
nonverbal communication, 59,
        128–129
nutrition, 119
nutritional supplements, 79–80

occipital frontalis muscle, 59
opponens pollicis muscle, 58
orbicularis oculi muscles, 60
orbicularis oris muscles, 60
origins and insertions, 18–19
overtraining, 98–100

overuse injuries, 88–90
oxygen use, 25–26, 72
oxytocin, 31–32

palpebrae muscles, 60
Parent Project Muscular
    Dystrophy, 159
passive stretching, 27
pectoralis minor muscle, 50–51
penile erections, 124
pennate muscles, 17
peristalsis, 49–50
physical therapy/therapists, 94,
    116–119
plantar fasciitis, 89
plantar flexion, 16
poliomyelitis (polio), 112
posture, muscles for, 53–54
potassium, 110
power, muscle, 35–36, 40–41
pronation, 16
prostheses, 139–140
protein production, 14
protraction, 15
psoas minor muscle, 120
pterygoid muscles, 46
pyloric sphincter, 50
pyomyositis, 112

quadratus lumborum, 51
quadricep muscles, 19, 36, 57

recreation and sports
    and body types, 131–132
    endurance training, 81
    flexibility training, 74–75
    injuries, 95–100
    muscle cramps, 91
    overtraining, 98–100
    R.E.S.T.S. injury prevention,
        102–103
    sprains and strains, 90
    stitches, 92

strength training, 70, 77–78
    tendinitis, 103
    torn rotator cuffs, 100–102
    See also exercise
rectus abdominis muscle, 54–55
reflexes, 61–62
REM sleep, 129
respiratory system, 66
R.E.S.T.S. prevention, 102–103
retraction, 15
rhabdomyolysis, 113–114
rhabdomyoma, 115
R.I.C.E. treatment, 90–91
rigor mortis, 141–142
risorious muscle, 59
rotation, 15
rotator cuffs, torn, 100–102

sarcolemma, 23
sarcomere, 22, 69–70
sarcopenia, 127–128
sartorius muscle, 17, 45
scalene muscles, 51
shin splints, 89
shivering, 14, 42
shoulder joint, 100–102
size, muscle, 33, 35, 70
skeletal muscle
    defined, 11, 12, 13
    movements, 14–16
    process of functioning, 18–20
    shapes, 17–18
skin muscles, 14
sleep and muscles, 129
sliding filament model, 21–24
smooth muscle, 124
    contraction, 31
    defined, 12, 13
soft palate, 48
soleus muscle, 30
space, muscles in, 143–147
speech and singing, 52–53
sperm maturation, 124

sports and recreation
    and body types, 131–132
    endurance training, 81
    flexibility training, 74–75
    injuries, 95–100
    muscle cramps, 91
    overtraining, 98–100
    R.E.S.T.S. injury prevention,
        102–103
    sprains and strains, 90
    stitches, 92
    strength training, 70, 77–78
    See also exercise
    torn rotator cuffs, 100–102
sprains and strains, 90
stabilizer muscles, 20
stapedius muscle, 33
stem cells, 138–139
steroids, anabolic, 84–87
stitches, muscle, 92
strength training, 70, 77–78
superior rectus muscle, 60
supination, 16
swallowing, 48–49
Swammerdam, Jan, 7–9
synchronous muscles, 43
synergist muscles, 20
synovial membranes, 18

temporalis muscle, 46
tendinitis, 103
tendons, 18, 20, 103, 136
tension-type headaches, 94–95
testosterone, 85, 133
tetanic contraction, 30
thumbs, 58
tics, muscle, 121
tone, muscle, 34
tongue muscles, 47, 52–53
Tour de France (cycling), 65–68
transplanting muscle, 135–136
transversus abdominis muscle,
    55

trichinellosis (trichinosis),
    112–113
Type I fibers, 29, 67–68
Type II fibers, 29–30

ultrastructural damage, 77
upper esophageal sphincter, 48
urethra, 56
urination, 56

vas deferens muscles, 124
vocal folds, 52
volume, muscle, 8–9
vomiting, 50

walking, 56–57
websites for information, 157
women and muscles, 133–134
work, 36
Works, Shari, 116–119

Z-line streaming, 71
zygomatic major muscle, 60